A LIFETIME OF LESSONS

MORE THAN 50 YEARS OF EXPERT INSTRUCTION TO HELP YOU PLAY YOUR BEST GOLF NOW

Marshall Smith
with David DeNunzio

TRIUMPH
BOOKS
CHICAGO

Library of Congress Cataloging-in-Publication Data

Smith, Marshall, 1926–
    A lifetime of lessons : more than 50 years of expert instruction to help you play your best
golf now / Marshall Smith with David Dinunzio.
        p. cm.
    ISBN-13: 978-1-57243-810-1
    ISBN-10: 1-57243-810-X
1.   Golf—Study and teaching. I. Dinunzio, David, 1968– II. Title.
    GV962.5.S63 2006
    796.35207—dc22

                                                        2005036355

This book is available in quantity at special discounts for your group or organization.
For further information, contact:

        Triumph Books
        542 South Dearborn Street
        Suite 750
        Chicago, Illinois 60605
        (312) 939-3330
        Fax (312) 663-3557

Printed in China
ISBN-13: 978-1-57243-810-1
ISBN-10: 1-57243-810-X

Cover design by Preston Pisellini
Cover photograph by Warren Keating
Page design and production by Robert Wyszkowski

All photographs taken on the Mountain Course at Robinson Ranch in Santa Clarita, California, by
Warren Keating, with the following exceptions: p. v, Ky Laffoon by BETTMAN/CORBIS; p. 35,
Gary Player by Getty Images; p. 46, spinning top by Royalty Free/CORBIS; p. 54, Dave Hill by
Getty Images; p. 72, Mickey Mantle by MLB Photos via Getty Images; p. 123, Lee Trevino
sequence courtesy of Werner Publishing.

Special thanks to instruction model Ryan Noll.

CONTENTS

PREFACE

LIKE EVERY YOUNG MAN DID AFTER THE END OF WORLD WAR II, I MADE MY WAY BACK HOME.

My family's insurance agency in Miami, Oklahoma, was there for me to take over, and I was excited to begin working and return to the golf courses I had missed so much during the war.

Quickly thereafter, I became friends with George Coleman. The Coleman family's interest ranged from automobile production to oil drilling and to lead and zinc mining, and George was an especially influential tycoon. In fact, during the war, he arranged employment for golf buddies Ben Hogan and Ky Laffoon under J. Paul Getty at Spartan Aeronautics in Tulsa, Oklahoma. George, Ben, Ky, and other great players of the day, such as Herman Kaiser and Ed Dudley, spent lots of time playing golf on the links of Oklahoma. The group eventually spearheaded the development of Southern Hills Country Club, which you'll likely recognize as the site of a few noteworthy U.S. Opens. I was lucky enough to receive an invitation to join them from time to time.

From the day we first met, Ky and I became great, great friends. In much the same way I foster some of the younger kids I teach today, Ky took me under his wing. Now, you can bet I had already thought I knew everything there was to know about golf, but Ky raised my understanding and love for golf to a wonderful new level. The fact that I even think I can write a golf book, and that you, the reader, are even remotely interested in what I have to say, can all be traced back to Ky.

Here's all you need to know about my very dear friend and mentor: he was the best golfer I ever saw. He never took home a major trophy, but you can believe that his peers, who included Gene Sarazen and Byron Nelson, always kept their eyes on the leader board whenever Ky's name appeared on the pairings sheet. In the 1930s alone, Ky finished second or first 65 times—not bad for a golfer you may have never heard of. Ky

Part American Indian, part golfing machine, and the most genuine man I have ever met, Ky Laffoon (posing here in Virginia Beach, Virginia, in 1935) was my very dear friend, mentor, and inspiration.

competed for our country in Ryder Cups and played in the first 10 Masters Tournaments.

You'll find accounts of Ky's outbursts and fierce emotions. And while it's true Ky wore whatever he was thinking—or feeling—on his sleeve, he was always a gentleman and respected the game more than any golfer I've known. Plus, if there's one thing that can be said about people such as Ky, it's that they're honest (wouldn't it be nice to have a few more of those around these days?). I'm sure you've read stories about Ky tying a putter to the back of his car and dragging it to the next tournament site if it ever let him down. Or how he was so fearful of letting his right hand take over his swing that he'd stick it in a rosebush, and then follow in with the left, "in case it had any ideas." Maybe you've heard that he stuffed his Cadillac with clothes, basically living out of his car, and filled the trunk with dozens of putters (many of them damaged) and a jar of peanut butter ("in case I got hungry").

Well, much of that is true. But that was just Ky being Ky, and if you knew him like I did, it was these types of antics that made you love him even more.

I owe the life I enjoy so emphatically to this outrageous golfing savant from Zinc, Arkansas. And there isn't a day that goes by without me thinking of him or one of the lessons he so graciously taught me. I wish the golfing public would open up more to his legacy. Who wouldn't enjoy a character like Ky on the PGA Tour today, a character who could back up his stage show with play that was rivaled by only three or four golfers during his prime?

Ky, this book is dedicated to you. I miss you and thank you so very much for giving me the tools to do what I do today so that your skills will be passed on to yet another generation of golfers who love the game as much as you did.

ACKNOWLEDGMENTS

I SUPPOSE NOW'S A GOOD TIME TO THANK EVERYONE WHO HELPED MAKE THIS BOOK POSSIBLE, BUT WHERE DO I BEGIN?

Thank you, my beautiful wife, Corinne—for everything. Some may call her a golf widow, but she's not. Corinne has always encouraged me to follow my passion, and I love her for that. Plus, whether I'm on the course, on the lesson tee, or at home with her watching Westerns, she's always in my heart. Likewise for all of our children and grandchildren. My, how I'm blessed.

TO MY GOOD FRIEND AND EDITOR AT *GOLF TIPS* MAGAZINE, DAVID DENUNZIO. Without David, this book would be 160 blank pages, and I'd have nowhere to stay when I come out to Los Angeles. Thanks, David—you're the best. And thanks to everyone at *Golf Tips*: Mike Chwasky, Ryan Noll, Dave Brennan, Warren Keating, Janet Gondo, Maggie Devcich, Connie Lee, Molly Kemp, Michael Young, and the Werner family.

TO MR. JAN RUSSO, a true New Yorker who got this project off the ground and running. What a great job, Jan. When we all needed that extra push, Jan provided a shove.

THANKS TO EVERYONE AT TRIUMPH BOOKS IN CHICAGO, especially Tom Bast, Linc Wonham, Fred Walski, Kelley White, and Amy Reagan. Watching y'all work almost makes me wish I were in the publishing business, not golf.

ALSO, TOM FERRELL, WITH WHOM I WROTE MY FIRST BOOK, and whose thoughts on my technique and lessons are featured throughout this text. Tom's from Georgia, and I just love it when two Southern boys can get together to produce something special.

LAST, TO EVERYONE I HAVE MET THROUGH GOLF—a sincere thank-you and God bless to all of my very best friends. The fact that you're reading this book makes you part of this group. I hope that one day you'll be able to stop by and say hi.

I love teaching at all levels, but there's nothing quite like the thrill of working with the best players in the world. I first met Todd Fischer at the Nationwide Tour's 2002 Fort Smith Classic and have been with him on the PGA Tour ever since.

Three-time winner Walt Zembriski and me in the early days of the Senior PGA Tour.

INTRODUCTION

WHEN I FIRST PICKED UP A GOLF CLUB, OUR GREAT COUNTRY HAD BEEN THROUGH ONLY ONE WORLD WAR. PROFESSIONAL GOLFERS STILL WORE PLUS-FOURS, AND IF AN AUTOMOBILE EVER CAME COUGHING DOWN COMMERCE STREET IN MY HOMETOWN OF MIAMI, OKLAHOMA, WELL, WE ALL RAN DOWN TO SEE WHAT ALL THE COMMOTION WAS ABOUT.

If I ever got the chance to head up to Baxter Springs, Kansas, and play Baxter Springs Country Club (my favorite nine-holer), I was sure to bring a two-by-four to smooth out the sand-and-oil greens before I attempted to putt. My woods were wooden, and the new steel shafts were all the rage. That was close to 70 years ago, but it truly seems like only yesterday.

If you're like me, you count the years in golf terms. My first birdie as a kid. My first sub-par round as a teenager. Playing competitive golf at Ol' Miss and Northeastern Oklahoma A&M as a collegian. Convincing my new bride that golf was just something I had to do on weekends (and some weekdays, too). Teaching my kids (and now my grandchildren) the game as an adult. And, ultimately, finding my niche as a tour instructor in my later years and writing this golf instruction book at a time when everyone says I should be winding down a little. Yes, every conceivable important moment in my life has been touched by golf. It has kept me young, and it has continually brought perspective to my life.

I didn't meet my wife, Corinne, in a nightclub or on the Internet. I was introduced by my best friend, Mickey Mantle, with whom I played the most rounds of golf, with the exception of my son, Marshall Jr. (who joined me in the Joplin Golf Hall of Fame in 2001). As owner

Me (left), Mickey Mantle (center), and Yankees pitcher Tom Sturdivant at Miami Country Club in 1958.

of an insurance company and a bank, I closed more deals between swings than I ever did in a suit and tie. If I ever wanted a match, I'd walk into Miami Country Club or Southern Hills and instantly find a friend ready for the challenge. It's always been that way. You may never have pegged northeastern Oklahoma as a golf mecca, but you'd be surprised at what's happened here over the years. Thanks to my neighbor and dear friend George Coleman, a local businessman, the likes of Ky Laffoon, Ben Hogan, and Ed Dudley

**Marshall Jr., Craig Stadler, and me at
Mickey's Celebrity Golf Tournament at Shangri-La Resort.**

I guess that's why I take the simple approach in teaching others how to play. K.I.S.S. is the name of the game (you'll learn more about this in chapter 1). To be honest, I never set out to become a golf instructor, let alone one for 50 years. When *Golf Tips* magazine approached me in 1996 to become a member of its instruction editorial staff, I was surprised to learn that they'd actually pay me to write stories. Half of the time I give lessons because that's what I know how to do. I suppose I'm a by-product of my environment. Miami (where I still reside) is a small place, and seemingly everyone is your friend. If you're eager to improve your golfing skills or simply anxious to learn the basic fundamentals of the game, you're my friend, too.

Many people ask, "If you know so much about golf, then how come you never were on tour or had big-time students?" Well, in my day, the tour was no place for a father of five and a husband. And in response to the student portion of the question, I think lending a hand to Chi Chi Rodriguez, Gary Player, Craig Stadler, and Walt Zembriski qualifies as big enough. Sure, I know I haven't marketed myself like other full-time instructors, but that's just not my style. Truth be told, I had the fortune of teaching a few famous folks here and there simply because they were my friends.

When you watch Tiger Woods with his pro, it's very businesslike. When I was working with Chi Chi, Craig, and Walt, there were more belly laughs than swing tips. Of course, we knew when it was time to get down to business, but whenever I think of these guys, I think of their smiles and not their swings. I sincerely hope you bring—or will learn to bring—that kind of attitude to your game.

With my current students, I feel I have fallen into a more fatherly role, which has worked out just fine. For these young players (most of whom have been swinging a club since they could walk and have undergone every type of analysis, modification, and swing overhaul imaginable), my simple approach to

(Augusta National's first head professional) made the Joplin, Missouri, and Miami, Oklahoma, areas their second homes at different parts of their lives.

One of my first young pupils was a Kansas kid by the name of Hale Irwin, who grew up on the aforementioned Baxter Springs Country Club. And in the off-season, Mickey would have nearly every big name in baseball over for matches at our very own Miami Country Club. His celebrity tournaments at local Shangri-La Resort were the stuff of legends. When Corinne and I thumb through some of our old photo albums, we can't believe our eyes—all these larger-than-life folk in little ol' Miami (pronounced Mi-am-uh, by the way, after the local Indian tribe). We have some nice courses here, but not anything that would attract A-list personnel. I think they came because golf here has always been about, well, golf. And despite all the famous people I've known and taught (even recently giving Bill Murray some lessons at Pauma Valley Country Club in San Diego, California, through my good friend Chad Petitt), golf has simplified my life and, in so doing, has enriched it beyond my wildest imaginations. Thank you, golf.

Famous or otherwise, I've always had a favorite student: Marshall Jr.

instruction is music to their ears. Often, they'll call from tournaments just to hear a little encouragement, like you used to pine for when you first went away to college or had brought your first baby home from the hospital. Todd Fischer, a four-year PGA Tour veteran here in 2006, doesn't need me to break down his plane switches. What he does need is a keen, seasoned eye to discover a nagging hitch that may have entered his already near-perfect technique and to simply say, "Go get 'em." Same thing goes for my kids on the lesser-known tours such as the Nationwide and Hooters. Amazingly, it applies to a lot of the big boys on the PGA Tour practice ranges, too. I hope it also finds favor with you.

Golf is simple, folks. All I have to do is trace back the past 70 years to remind me of that fact. I played some of my best rounds when what mattered most was the camaraderie between me and the other members of my foursome. I think back to the time when Mickey and I were still young, when he could

hit the ball farther than anyone and how he still couldn't beat the man in the bucket hat. I remember meeting all the great people in my life through golf. I can see myself shaking hands on the course with all of my soon-to-be lifelong friends for the first time—George Coleman, Otis Winter, Steve Owens, Bill Grigsby, Dale McNamara, and every single pupil—though I couldn't possibly tell you what I scored that day. If you ponder long and hard enough, I'm sure you'll begin to feel the same way. In every other sport, score is paramount. In golf, we keep score, but the scores darken against the bright light of the awesome memories the game provides.

I love golf. I love my family. I am so very grateful for all that each has brought to my life. The game has taught me a lot about life and about myself. These have been golf's true lessons, though I'll give you all you need in the next hundred pages or so to take your game to levels you may have not believed possible. Don't worry—better golf is just around the corner.

I never thought I'd ever write an instruction book. Honestly, I'd rather you'd just pop into Miami, Oklahoma, and knock on my door for a lesson (anyone can give you directions). But here we are, and boy, am I excited. To think all of this can be chalked up to a chance meeting at a bar with golf writer Tom Ferrell at the 1996 PGA Convention in Las Vegas. I was there to support my dear friend Dick De La Cruz and his club designs for Goldwin Golf. As one beer led to another, Tom convinced me that I had something to say and that there were lots of people—people fed up with teaching fads and stagnant indexes—who were waiting to listen. I hope you enjoy this book. I certainly have enjoyed everything in the past 70 years that led up to it.

**K.I.S.S.: KEEP IT SIMPLE STU—
WELL, YOU KNOW THE REST**

1

I'VE NEVER SEEN ANYBODY—AND THAT INCLUDES BEN HOGAN, JACK NICKLAUS, AND TIGER WOODS—WHO WAS SO GOOD AT GOLF THAT HE OR SHE DIDN'T NEED ANY HELP WITH HIS OR HER GAME.

The problem is, where do you draw the line? I've seen players from beginners to superstars make the mistake of becoming hooked on teachers. The bottom line is that golf is an individual game and no one can do it for you. There's no pinch-hitting in golf. Teachers are businesspeople just like you. They're looking for repeat customers. They'll get you on video and give you a long list of drills that you're supposed to work on between visits. While I believe that most instructors are sincere in wanting to help their students, I see them creating dependencies that end up hurting the golfer in the long run. If that's the case, then why should you spend time reading this book? We'll get to that in a moment.

Like I said, everyone can use a little help, and that's where I come in. God gave me a gift in that I can see the golf swing in very simple terms. I don't care who you are or how well you play, I can spot the one or two (sometimes three) big items you should work on in just a few minutes. Then it's up to you. If you allow me to take longer than 30 minutes with you on the lesson tee, then you're letting me steal your money. The best lessons are simple reminders. They reinforce what you already know, and they break down the complications that creep into your golf game and let you get back to the simple motion of swinging a golf club and making the ball do what you want it to do, no matter how long the shot.

That's the basis for my teaching philosophy—simplicity. The problem with most golf instruction is that it makes what should be a simple game very difficult. How many times have you duffed a shot, dropped a second ball, and then hit a shot even a tour pro would have been proud of? The reason is because you didn't put any pressure on yourself the second time around—you kept it simple. You stopped thinking about how to swing and you simply swung. "Hit your second shot first" is the best piece of advice I've ever received. That's why I'm giving it to you now.

For an even better example of golf at its simplest best, watch a child swing. It's amazing. I can't tell you how many parents have come up to me over the years claiming their son or daughter is the next Ernie Els or Annika Sorenstam. The fact is every child has a great swing. The reason is that they have yet to become polluted, inundated, and oversaturated by swing thoughts and worries such as right elbow position. They just rear back and swing with as much force as their little muscles can muster. It's pure motion, and if you don't think it's simple, ask the child how they do it. They won't have an answer. They just do it.

> **"'Hit your second shot first' is the best piece of advice I've ever received. That's why I'm giving it to you now."**

I've been in the golf instruction business a long time now. I've taught beginners, juniors, and players on the PGA, LPGA, and Champions Tours. My philosophy is K.I.S.S.—Keep It Simple Stupid.

I've seen swing fads come and go. I've seen flat swings, fast swings, and upright swings. I've read *The Golfing Machine* theories, studied Natural Golf

techniques, and seen enough training aids to fill a garbage dumpster. If you boil it all down, there's only one thing that all good golfers have in common, and that's balance. If you're looking for a secret, there it is. If you can combine power and balance, you can hit the ball long and straight. Sounds easy enough, right? It is, but it takes discipline and commitment to train your body to make a simple, balanced move during the golf swing. You have to master the fundamentals we'll discuss in this book, and once you do, you'll be on your way to enjoying a game that will last a lifetime. In other words, you'll come to love golf the way I do.

When I learned the game, instruction was different from what it is today. Players like Ky Laffoon, Sam Snead, Lloyd Mangrum, and Ben Hogan practiced "feel." They concerned themselves with knowing where the clubhead was during the swing. They didn't worry so much about looks. I think that's still the best way.

Today, too many instructors see the golf swing as a sequence of positions. You'll never be able to feel it that way, Try this simple exercise. Go get a sheet of paper and a pen. Now draw a circle. Did you draw the circle by starting and stopping through a series of arcs? Of course not! If you did, you'd see that it's not a very good circle—it's full of obvious breaks and sure to be a little lopsided. Instead, you just made a single motion and drew a circle on the page. Simple. I want you to think of the golf swing as a circle and the club as a pen in your hands.

This is why I don't use video analysis when I teach. It's easy to sit down and point out flaws on a video. But it doesn't always help the students. Like a circle, a good golf swing is one continuous motion, back and through. Your mind can't "freeze-frame" in the middle of the swing. If it does, I'll bet the farm that the results won't be very good. As you read through this book, you'll find that I do break down the swing position by position. But don't become enamored with fitting your swing into these ideals. Use the fundamentals within to create your own fluid motion. That's the key.

Take a minute to think about all the great athletes in any sport. Have you ever watched Peyton Manning throw a football? Does he make a long, conscious series of movements with his arm? No. He drops back, spots his target, sets his body, and throws the ball with a simple cock-and-release motion. Now, take a great pitcher like Greg Maddux. He makes a simple windup, moving his weight to his right side and then transferring to his left and delivering the ball. It's true with any sport. A great boxer throws lightning-quick punches because he keeps his preparations simple. Think about how you walk. There's no thought involved. You just take a stride that keeps you in balance, and away you go. That's the way a good golf swing is. You take basic fundamentals and apply them in a simple, well-balanced motion. If you don't get anything else out of this book, I want you to understand that.

Golf isn't a game you can master. Even the greatest players of all time knew that very early in their careers. That's part of its beauty, though. When the magic settles on you for a day on the golf course, it's like an angel reaching down from the clouds. What I want you to do is create the conditions that help the magic happen. As I tell my students, only one person has ever mastered the golf swing, and you can find him in the state asylum. Don't become crazed for perfection.

Of course, there's a lot more to hitting a golf ball well and posting good scores. Golf is a bond, the center of a community to which you'll always belong—as long as you love the game. I've been teaching since the Eisenhower Administration, and I never get tired of seeing students do something that they didn't think they could do. Everyone who has ever worked to learn the game understands golf's beauty and difficulty, as well as the commitment it takes to continue to improve. Watch two golfers—young and old, man and woman,

midhandicapper and tour pro—talk about the game. You'll see that the connection goes much deeper than a secret handshake or some crazy lodge greeting. The game brings people together. Once you get started, know that you're in it for life. A casual golfer is not a golfer. A golfer engrosses himself or herself as deeply into practicing and improving as they do playing.

Golf has opened so many doors for me. I've gotten to know wonderful people from all around the globe. I work with children and senior citizens, and through golf I know that in their hearts people are all the same, no matter how they look or how old they are. If you play golf, the greatest gift that you can give somebody is a love of the game. When you do that, you give a lasting gift that the recipient will never forget. You make yourself a part of the community—a chapter in this fantastic story.

In this book I'll share with you some of what I've learned over the past half century or so. Not just about golf swings and the techniques that can help you become a better player, but about the way golf's been a part of my life and what it has helped me to do.

We'll spend some time on the lesson tee, then head out to the course for all kinds of talk about playing golf, from managing your game to controlling your emotions to having good etiquette so that other people will enjoy playing with you. We'll work on practicing so that you can keep on learning and teaching yourself.

Too many players sign up for lessons and then work on nothing but the long game. In this book, we'll spend a lot of time on the short game, then work up to longer swings. That's because the short game breaks down the golf swing to its simple fundamentals, and that's where the learning begins. It's also because you hit two out of every three shots from inside 60 yards.

As we work, remember that you have to judge lessons by what you can take out on the golf course with you. These reminders should get you thinking right. If you can then work on keeping these motions simple, you'll be able to transfer your thinking to the golf course. Here's a good way to judge lessons: if it only works on the range, it's not worth your time or money.

I hope you can use some of these observations to enjoy golf more and to help others enjoy it as well. That's what it's all about. It's just that simple.

2

I BET YOU'RE WONDERING WHY I'M STARTING THE LESSON PORTION OF THIS BOOK WITH THE SHORT GAME.

Most golf instruction books and magazines emphasize the iron swing and, even more prominently, driving. Moreover, the short game (consisting of pitch and chip shots and greenside bunker play) is often viewed as simply a shorter version of the full swing act—an afterthought to the guts of your golf game. After all, if you can execute a fundamentally solid full swing with your 7 iron, then one with your sand wedge from 40 yards out should be a breeze, right? Wrong.

Standard instruction outlets aren't the only ones to blame for the short game's B-list status. You're at fault as well. I bet—if you're like most golfers I've met—you rate your game mostly by how good your long shots are. That's the wrong way to look at it. Sure, it's thrilling to bust a big drive or groove a long iron stiff to the pin, and I wouldn't dare suggest that hitting the ball well isn't an important part of developing a consistent golf game. But ball-striking is messy business. Some days you have the magic, and other days you don't. There's not much difference in a swing that sends the ball soaring on target and one that sends shots just a little bit off-line. That's why the short game is so important.

If your golf game had superheroes, the short game would be Clark Kent. At first glance, it's nothing special. After all, we're just talking about short little mild-mannered swings and shots that travel 100 yards or less. But when you're in trouble on the golf course—and everybody gets into trouble out there—your short game becomes Superman, helping you out of tough situations and saving your score on days when your long game just isn't quite right. Better yet, you don't even need a telephone booth to make it all happen.

I start every lesson with the short game. Let me say that again: I start every lesson with the short

game. It doesn't matter if I'm teaching a group of beginning golfers or one of my tour students. If you can learn to turn three shots into two, you'll become the best player you can be. Need proof? Just look at the stats from the professional circuits. Even the very best players average only 12 or 13 greens in regulation per round. As such, if they want to get in position to win tournaments, they must save par with the wedges. And on the days when they're swinging well and hitting the ball straight, wedges put them into position for birdies and ultra-low scores.

Improving your short game is the fastest and best way to improve your scoring. The more you simplify your approach to getting up and down by using old-fashioned horse sense around the greens, the better your chances of saving your par.

Here are the lessons I've used over the years to help my students improve their pitching, chipping, and bunker play.

LESSON 1: THE FULL WEDGE SWING

Golf isn't about perfection. I've been teaching golf for more than 50 years, long enough to know that it's a game of patience and recovery. That's what makes the short game so important. A good short game will get you safely through a day of mediocre ball-striking. By developing a short game that you can trust, you'll take pressure off of yourself, and you'll always have the chance to save a stroke. Those strokes add up. The problem is that most golfers make the short game too complicated. What you should really do with your short game—as with so many other areas of your life—is apply the K.I.S.S. rule.

I have an old saying: show me a guy who hits it two feet from the pin all day, and I'll show you a great putter. That's partially true, but the real short-game master

SOME GOOD ADVICE: "START WITH YOUR SAND WEDGE"

IN INSTRUCTION LORE, THERE'S NO GREATER STORY THAN BYRON Nelson accepting a visit from a young Tom Watson who, at the time, was hampered by an errant driver. Eager to show Mr. Nelson his flawed swing, Watson yanked his driver from his bag and set up to hit. Before he could start his backswing, Nelson stopped him, reached over to Watson's bag, pulled out the sand wedge, and handed it to Tom. "If you can show me you can swing the sand wedge correctly," Nelson quipped, "I'll let you hit your driver." If you're a beginner and reading this book, heed Nelson's advice and perfect your wedge swing before moving up to your longer clubs. The short-shot swing sets a great tempo for all full swings and is the foundation of your technique. Even to more experienced players I suggest you refocus your efforts on your wedges. The dividends will be immense, I assure you.

is the one who can put it two feet away on the proper side of the hole. When preparing to play a short shot, always designate a target area that will leave you with the easiest putt to complete the up and down. Generally, this should be below the hole so that you'll have a straightforward uphill putt that will allow you to be aggressive.

In order to select the target area, use any knowledge you have gained about the speed, slope, and grain of the greens. Knowing how these factors will affect the ball will help you determine the shot with the greatest chance of finding the target area.

Remember, on extremely fast, sloping greens, a two-foot downhill putt may be much more difficult than a five-foot uphill putt. Define your target area accordingly.

THE SETUP

1. RIGHT SHOULDER POSITIONED LOWER THAN THE LEFT.

2. HANDS NEUTRAL OR SLIGHTLY FORWARD PRESSED.

3. WEIGHT PRESET IN RIGHT HIP.

4. SHOULDER-WIDTH STANCE WITH FRONT FOOT FLARED SLIGHTLY.

5. BALL PLAYED SLIGHTLY BACK OF MIDDLE.

A good setup paves the way for a good shot. Start by gripping the club with both hands. Most of the grip pressure comes from the back two fingers of the left hand and the front two of the right hand. Your hands are crucial to a good short game, so make sure that they stay firm through the swing and don't "flip" the clubhead at the ball.

Stand up tall, between 12 and 18 inches from the ball, with your hands high and the club in an upright position. This emphasizes the feel of your hands and fingers and quiets the body. Your head should be slightly behind the ball, and your left shoulder should be raised so that your body is set like an airplane coming in for a landing.

Align your body so that you're square to the clubface. Remember, the clubface controls the trajectory and direction of the shot. Too many golfers open up the face of the wedge. I prefer to keep it square when I can, or even hood it a little bit. As you align with the target, use the entire leading edge of the clubface. If you align using just the sweet spot of the wedge,

"Hug" with a Wedge

WHEN HITTING A full wedge, keep one thing in mind: you're not hitting your driver or 4 iron. It's a relatively slow swing that emphasizes control over power. Furthermore, it's mostly an upper-body-dominated motion requiring little, if any, lower-body movement. Your setup should reflect these truths. For starters, hug the ball at address. Your wedges are the shortest clubs in your bag, so naturally you should stand closer to the ball.

"Reach" with the Driver

Also, it's a good idea to keep your right elbow close to your right side, which further emphasizes the need to hug the ball. Allow your arms to dangle from the shoulders and grip the club from there, with your hands just in front of your zipper. At the very least, let the lie of the wedge (the steepest of any club in the bag) dictate the placement of your hands, which naturally will be closer to your body.

you'll almost always open the clubface. Your stance should be no more than shoulder width, with the ball slightly back of middle.

When I worked with Chi Chi Rodriguez and showed him how to line up using the entire leading edge of the clubface, he told me that in all of his years playing he had never thought of that. And he quickly became an even better wedge player.

The key to a successful short-shot takeaway is to use your right elbow as your guide. That's why I ask all of my students—professional or otherwise—to set up to the ball with the right elbow close to the right side or at the very least, inside the left elbow. As you take away the club, that right elbow shouldn't move either forward or closer to your hip, just straight back, away

THE TAKEAWAY

1. STEADY HEAD AND UPPER BODY.

2. CLUB PUSHED BACK WITH LEFT SHOULDER.

3. CLUBSHAFT LYING ABOVE TOE LINE WITH CLUBHEAD POINTING SKYWARD.

4. RELAXED LOWER BODY.

from the target until it naturally hinges. The key is to push the club away from the ball with your left shoulder, moving in unison with your arms. It's an easy move that keeps the club on plane and in position to arrive at the ball on the proper path.

50-YEAR TIP: "KEEP THE CLUB OUT IN FRONT"

On Plane

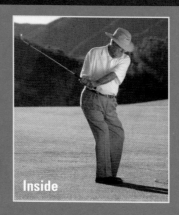
Inside

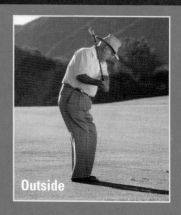
Outside

T HIS IS A BIG ONE. WHEN TAKING AWAY THE CLUB, NEVER EVER LET IT GET BEHIND YOUR RIGHT hip. If it does become trapped, there's just not enough time or speed in the wedge swing to reroute the club back on plane like there sometimes is with a long iron or driver swing. If you whip the club to the inside, it's likely it will stay there. Expect a lot of pushes, fat shots, and results short and right of your target. Expect the opposite if you take away the club too far to the outside. You know you've done it correctly when the shaft remains in front of your body all the way to the top. If it's not in front, it likely will be behind, and that's not what you want.

AT THE TOP

1. LEFT SHOULDER TURNING UNDERNEATH CHIN.

2. NINETY-DEGREE ANGLE BETWEEN LEFT FOREARM AND SHAFT.

3. WEIGHT FULLY TRANSFERRED TO RIGHT HIP.

4. LOWER BODY GROUNDED—LEFT FOOT REMAINS PLANTED.

The short-game swing is all about tempo and speed. Most people take too big a backswing and decelerate through impact, and that's the one thing that will kill any short shot. I've never seen anyone hit the ball with a backswing. When you make a long backswing, it means that everything else has to be perfect, and that's a risk you don't need when trying to get up and down.

My recommendations on the short-game stroke are to choke down and make a shorter swing, with the hands rarely swinging beyond shoulder height. Break your left wrist as you take the club away, keeping your right elbow close to your side. By setting your wrists early, you'll get the club up into a good position to come down and through the ball cleanly.

50-YEAR TIP: "WATCH YOUR WEIGHT"

IF YOU REALLY WANT TO IMPROVE YOUR WEDGE shots—all shots, actually—then it's important you keep your weight under control. I've instructed professional basketball players and horse jockeys, junior girls and offensive linemen, and seen them all have difficulty with properly shifting weight, regardless of their size. The absolute worst thing you can do in golf is to move your weight target-ward on the takeaway (photo below). Do yourself a favor and preset your weight a bit in your right hip at address. No, it's not cheating. In fact, it's one of the best things you can do for your swing, especially on shorter shots.

THE DOWNSWING

1. CHECK OUT THE HEAD—ROCK SOLID.

2. HANDS AND ARMS LEADING THE CLUB INTO THE HITTING ZONE.

3. WEIGHT MOVING ONTO RIGHT SIDE.

From the top, the worst thing you can do is panic. With a wedge, many golfers feel they don't have enough energy stored to hit the ball the desired distance. Trust me, you do. With a wedge shot, centered contact is more important than speed. So, at the top, be patient: don't rush the downswing. In fact, during your practice, take the club to the end of the backswing and pause. Then begin your downswing, which, like the backswing, is fueled by the arms and hands. Remember, your lower body and left side are already turned out of the way. If you'd like, focus on moving your hands along the same route they took away from the ball.

Notice how I've failed to mention the head. That's done purposely, for in a good wedge swing, the head remains back, relatively still, and always remains between your shoulders. If you're prone to shanking your short shots, the culprit might be your head. In a shank, the club at impact is closer to the ball than it was at address. If you move your head down, your body, arms, and shaft will follow. Now the hosel is in the way. Same goes if you typically strike short shots thinly. This time, your head is moving up. Keep your head steady and allow your right shoulder to move fluidly underneath it.

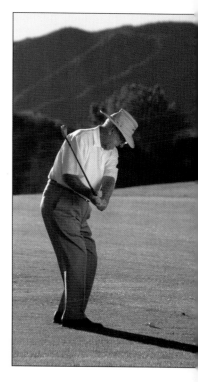

The most important thing to remember about the downswing is not to rush it. Only when the club is fully set at the top—regardless of the length of the backswing—should you make your move back down to the ball.

50-YEAR TIP: "DROP IT"

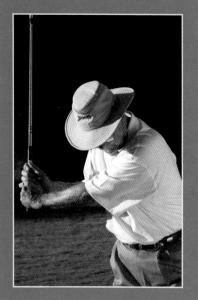

IF YOU REALLY WANT TO MAKE simple work of your wedge swing, let your hands lead. By that I mean from the top, power them downward before executing your turn toward the target. Popularly know as "finding the slot," dropping the hands first then following this drop by turning your shoulders then your hips is critical for top-level contact. All good wedge contact occurs from a descending blow, and if you fail to drop the hands at the start of the downswing, you'll produce more of a sweep across the ball. Remember, it's all in your hands.

IMPACT

1. THE HEAD STILL REMAINS BEHIND THE BALL.

2. FOREARM AND HAND ARRANGEMENT SIMILAR TO ADDRESS POSITION.

3. NO LIFTING OFF THE BACK FOOT—SOLID, GROUNDED CONTACT.

4. NICE DIVOT, EVIDENCE OF SWINGING "DOWN AND THROUGH."

By now, you've already taken a lot of guesswork out of the process. The only real goal at impact is to hit the ball squarely on the clubface. If you've prepared well, the rest will take care of itself.

When you walk, you just put one foot in front of the other. You don't make a long, complicated motion. That's the rhythm you want on your short shots. Then you just keep your head behind the ball and concentrate on contacting the ball first. There—it's not that complicated.

Watch any tour player make a short-game swing, and one thing should jump out: the legs of the golfer are dead. The smooth, unhurried, even tempo of a short swing doesn't require a ton of leg action. In fact, if you set up properly with a slightly open stance, you shouldn't need any leg action at all.

Above all, don't shift laterally or flail your hips open as if you're trying to crush the ball 300 yards. The short game is all about control, so stay in control and keep those legs quiet. Plus, because wedge shots require a shorter, slower swing, there isn't enough time to maneuver the hips closed, then open, before impact.

THE MOST IMPORTANT move in the downswing is to move your right shoulder toward the target and under your chin. If you keep it behind the chin (away from the target), you'll create either an early release or an ugly-looking scoop motion. Be careful not to simply turn your shoulders—this easily can lead to pulls. The right shoulder turns, but it turns down the target line. Guess what's in the way? Your chin. Now you get the idea.

THE RELEASE

1. HEAD "RIDING" WITH THE SWING, YET STILL BEHIND THE BALL.

2. RIGHT SHOULDER CONTINUES TO MOVE UNDER THE CHIN AND THROUGH TO THE TARGET.

3. LEFT-HAND KNUCKLES ARE VISIBLE, WHICH IS A GREAT INDICATION OF PROPER CLUBFACE ROTATION.

4. LEFT LEG "POSTING" TO RECEIVE WEIGHT.

5. FEET REMAIN GROUNDED.

Although contact with the ball already has been made, continue to focus on tempo. These shots are all about timing. Don't try to help the ball get airborne. Instead, try to feel the ball walk up the grooves of the club. When you're hitting good wedge shots it will seem as if the ball stays on the clubface forever.

Your finish should take care of itself—just let your hands release naturally. I like to imagine reaching out to shake hands with a friend at the end of the swing. This helps me be sure to swing all the way through. Pose at the end of your wedge shots on the range, holding the finish until the ball lands. You'll get a feel for the balance and rhythm of the shot—and your body naturally will work to re-create it.

As you'll discover in a few pages, I always have my students hit a few shots with just their right hands to get the tempo of the swing. Sometimes I'll have them count out the backswing and downswing or simply hum a favorite tune. The key is tempo and rhythm when you have a short club in your hands.

"Don't try to help the ball get airborne. Instead, try to feel the ball walk up the grooves of the club."

Sliding or overusing the legs on the downswing (left) forces an unbalanced finish (right).
On the other hand, a smooth, controlled rotation through to the target (left photo on next page) produces a
balanced end of the swing (right photo on next page). Remember to pose for the camera!

50-YEAR TIP: "SHAKE HANDS"

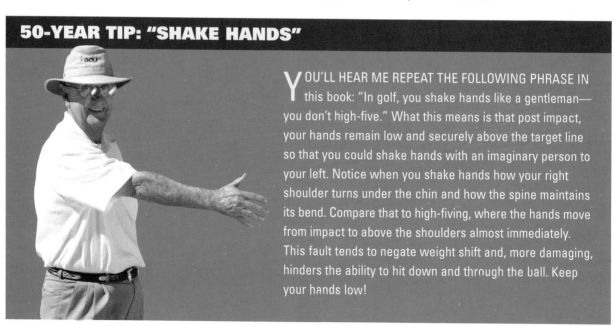

YOU'LL HEAR ME REPEAT THE FOLLOWING PHRASE IN this book: "In golf, you shake hands like a gentleman—you don't high-five." What this means is that post impact, your hands remain low and securely above the target line so that you could shake hands with an imaginary person to your left. Notice when you shake hands how your right shoulder turns under the chin and how the spine maintains its bend. Compare that to high-fiving, where the hands move from impact to above the shoulders almost immediately. This fault tends to negate weight shift and, more damaging, hinders the ability to hit down and through the ball. Keep your hands low!

THE FINISH

We all know what a good finish looks and feels like. Yet it's impossible to force a proper finish. In other words, a golfer can't proceed to make a bunch of mistakes in the downswing and expect to end up in a solid, balanced finish position. Try making a cake using the wrong ingredients and you'll see what I mean.

Proper technique fuels a proper finish, and there's no greater relationship between a good finish and a good technique than weight transfer. If you mismanage your weight or you slide instead of turning during your downswing, your chances of settling into a nice, balanced finish decrease.

Let's keep things simple, folks: keep your feet on the ground. Sounds straightforward, but you'd be amazed by how many people actually lift their left foot on the backswing and rise up on the toes of their right on the downswing. Remember, we're talking about the wedge swing—that smooth, controlled,

relatively slow motion where accuracy reigns supreme. Instead of "toe dancing," keep your feet grounded, and focus on the movement of weight in your feet rather than movement of the feet themselves. Feel your weight move to the right foot on the backswing (toward the heel), evenly to the middle of each foot on the downswing, then toward the heel of the left foot post impact. Stay grounded! Doing so will also help you hit down and through as you should. Your right foot shouldn't lose contact with the ground until the force of your swing naturally pulls it up into a balanced finish.

Also, as your right shoulder swings underneath your chin, allow your head to rotate along with it. This move facilitates shifting weight to the left side, helps keep the spine angle intact, and better allows the right shoulder to move toward the target. As the ball sails away, you should be able to track its flight with your left eye looking firmly down the target line.

THE FULL WEDGE SWING: PUTTING IT ALL TOGETHER

1. YOU NEED . . . TO OPEN UP

The wedge swing normally is not a full-swing shot, so it needs special attention at the setup. Because there isn't enough time in the wedge swing to get your left side out of the way and shift weight to your front foot, set your weight forward at address and adopt a slightly open stance. Now all you need to do is take the club back and through (without rushing or overaccelerating). To guarantee centered contact, hitch your right elbow to your side and keep it there until impact. This is an effective way to keep the club on plane and make clean, crisp contact with the golf ball.

While your driver swing and wedge swing should take the same amount of time to complete (tempo, tempo), don't fail to understand that a wedge swing is slower and, therefore, doesn't need a ton of lower-body action to power the club into impact. Watch any good wedge player and you'll see him or her keep everything below the knees fairly quiet. That being said, you can't execute a sound wedge swing without opening up your hips to your target on the downswing. So how do you open up if you're meant to keep the lower body still? At address, gently pull the front foot back so your hips are a bit open to the target. With the hips preset in this open position, all that's left to do is power the club back and through with the arms and shoulders.

2. YOU NEED . . . TO UNDERSTAND SPIN

Many of my students ask how they can add more spin to their wedge shots. Adding spin is key—it affords yet another option from short distances. Typical instruction says that in order to add spin you must "pinch" the ball against the turf. That's true, but in trying to create the pinch, most golfers simply speed up on the downswing—a huge no-no. The first step is

to understand how spin is created. Spin results from the ball "rolling" up the clubface, a phenomenon affected by the size and depth of your grooves. The more the ball rolls up the face, the more it will spin. It makes sense, then, that for more spin, ball contact should be made lower on the face, giving the ball more time to roll up the grooves. Enter scoring lines two and three: for the most spin, create contact near the bottom grooves rather than those in the middle or toward the top. Usually when I offer this advice, students scull the ball. Crucial to this technique is striking the ball with a descending blow. In a good wedge swing, the club moves down and through (see photo on this page). If it only moves down, be prepared for a fat shot. If it only moves through, expect to hit your next chip from beyond the other side of the green.

3. YOU NEED . . . DISTANCE CONTROL

The plethora of multiple wedge offerings is fantastic. They've made extinct the old saying, "A sand wedge is the only wedge a good player needs." That adage came from Greg Norman, who I bet has added a lob wedge to his set since. Nevertheless, despite owning the tools for hitting any number of specific yardages from 125 yards and in, most short shots you'll face will require something much different than a full swing from one of the two or three wedges in your bag.

Let's imagine a 30-yard shot. If the pin were up, I'd opt to open the face and hit a high shot that drops and stops immediately upon landing. If the pin is back, then I'd closed the face and hit a lower shot, planning to land short of the pin to let the ball run to the hole after it lands. Either way, I make the same swing with only a slight change in backswing length.

This seems to be where most recreational players have difficulty. Maybe this bit of advice will help. For the first shot, the 30-yard high-lofter, I take my hands back to my waist. For the lower shot, I stop my backswing at my knees. From these two 30-yard options, I can build back-

30-Yard Swing

60-Yard Swing

90-Yard Swing

swings to match varying lengths. Say the shot is 60 yards. To hit it high, I open the clubface and take my hands back to shoulder level; for the low runner, I'll stop my hands at my waist. And if I need to hit the shot full, well, I'll just execute my regular ol' full backswing.

The next time you practice, bring only your sand wedge. Pick a target 30 yards away. Open the face and see how far a backswing you need to land the ball that distance. Next close the face and see just how much you need to shorten your backswing to hit the same yardage. It's a perfect way to learn distance control and improve your wedge swing at the same time. In a single practice session, you'll groove a feel for specific yardages without much effort.

4. YOU NEED . . . FACE CONTROL

What if I were to tell you that it's possible to handle any short-yardage situation from 85 yards and in with a single swing? Wouldn't that be nice? Well, that's certainly a reality. You can create different trajectories and distances from a single swing by simply learning to open and close the face of your sand wedge. Maybe Norman was right; a sand wedge is the only wedge a good player really needs. The key is to control the face. Here's how.

With a grooved sand-wedge swing, you now have all you need to hit a variety of distances and to produce varying trajectories. Opening or closing the face at address accomplishes this. For less distance and more

Open Face

Neutral Face

Closed Face

Not only can different clubs and different backswing lengths produce different shot distances, so, too, can opening or closing the clubface. Opening the face effectively adds loft to the club, increasing the height of the shot while reducing distance. Closing the face reduces loft, producing a lower, longer shot with the same club.

loft, rotate the face open. For more distance or to produce a lower trajectory, simply close the face.

When opening or closing the face, never look at the center of the club. Doing so can give you an inaccurate reading of just how far open or closed you've rotated the face. Instead, look to the toe. Imagine a line running from your stance line through the hosel. How does that line look at the toe? If it's left of the toe, then the face is open. If it's right, then the face is closed.

For both open- and closed-face shots, use the same stance described previously. Of course, the more you open the face, the more left of target you should align your feet at address, and vice versa for closed-face shots. Regardless, both shots require a slightly open stance with the majority of weight situated over the front hip and leg.

5. YOU NEED . . . TO TAKE INVENTORY

If there's one thing for certain in golf, it's that you rarely face the same exact shot twice in a round. The full-swing wedge shot we're discussing here could be 100 yards, 70, or maybe 77. Furthermore, you should never find yourself adding speed, or applying the brakes, to any swing to dictate how far you hit the golf ball. Shot distance with your short clubs—for all clubs, really—is dictated by the length of your backswing, not

speed or tempo. Remember, tempo is a constant in golf; backswing length isn't. It's therefore critical that you spend time and, for each wedge in your set, know how far you hit with 50 percent, 75 percent, and 100 percent backswing lengths.

There's nothing wrong with taking notes. Make an inventory of shot distances with varying backswing lengths. For instance, I hit a 50 percent sand wedge 60 yards. It's also the same distance as my 75 percent lob shot. See? Now I have options, and, more important, I have the means to hit the golf ball the exact distance the shot requires.

How many times, from 75 yards, have you come up 15 yards short or 15 yards long? I bet it's more than you'd like to admit. Erring by that much from such short distance is unforgivable. Good wedge players know how to hit the ball specific distances. The key is practice.

Use a session on the range to find out how far you hit each wedge with backswings that stop at the knee, the waist, and the shoulder. Once you have this inventory of shots, you'll know how far to take the club back when you're faced with a specific yardage on the course. Remember, the length of your backswing, not the force of your swing, controls how far you hit a wedge. Set the length, and then accelerate through impact.

	PW DISTANCE (yds)	GW DISTANCE (yds)	SW DISTANCE (yds)	LW DISTANCE (yds)
25%	30	25	20	15
50%	65	50	40	30
75%	90	75	60	45
Full	125	100	80	65

LESSON 2: CHIP SHOTS

A good chip-shot player is usually a good lag putter as well. That's because he or she understands how to use the speed, slope, and grain of the green to his or her advantage. You should start any short-game practice by getting a feel for the greens you'll be playing that day. Spend a few minutes on the putting green before you move over to the pitching and chipping area. The idea is to get a feel for how the ball will behave when it's rolling on the ground. A small investment in learning the tendencies of the greens will pay off many times over on the golf course.

Know the geography: is there a geographical feature that affects the ball consistently? In the mountains, for instance, the ball will often tend to break away along a certain ridge. On seaside courses, it will move toward the ocean. My friends on the tour always make a mental note of how the land drains and use it to their advantage.

Know the grain of the green: this is particularly important on Bermuda grass, but it's a factor on every course. Go to the center of the putting green and roll several balls toward the fringe in each direction. See how the different putts behave, and note the effect of the grain on each one. If you ever have the opportunity to watch a PGA Tour event practice round, you'll see the players doing exactly that on each green.

As far as shot selection is concerned, the most important thing is not to get fancy. Don't try a highlight-film flop shot when a nice little chip would do the job just as well. Use club selection to help with this. The basic idea is to use the chip technique for any shot. If you need to hit it higher, take a sand wedge or a lob wedge. You'll naturally get more loft without having to make major adjustments to your stroke. For more roll, go to a less-lofted iron. Sometimes it's easier to roll a ball up onto the green than it is to fly it onto a ledge with little margin for error. Work backward from your target area, and go with the shot that makes the most sense—not the one that will most impress your playing partners.

THERE ARE REALLY ONLY THREE CHOICES WHEN it comes to getting the ball close to the hole from short distance—a chip, a pitch, or a lob. I advise my students, from bogey golfers to tour players, to keep the ball low to the ground whenever possible. The sooner you can get the ball rolling on the green, the sooner you're on a predictable surface that will accommodate a less-than-perfect shot. Now that's using the K.I.S.S. philosophy.

MY CHIP SHOT TECHNIQUE

Of all the shots in golf, chip shots are my favorite. I've literally spent years of my life chipping—in the backyard, with my kids, against friends at the club in friendly competitions, and alone around the practice green with the setting sun as my only companion. Chips are funny: they're not full swings, but they're not putts, either. They're kind of a blend and therefore require a special technique. Here's what I focus on.

I try to settle into a relaxed address position, just slightly opening my stance by pulling back my left foot. I play the ball back with my hands forward-pressed. This assures that I make a nice "pop" on the ball. Scooping need not apply when it's time to chip.

To take away the club, I use my hands and never—ever—move my hands above my knee. The clubhead should remain low to the ground until a slight—slight—hinge of the wrists brings the club up (below, left).

Before I change direction, I ease up on my hold of the club just a bit. The sensation I want to create is that my hands lead the club back to the ball, but they don't dominate to the point where they overtake it. The last thing you want in a chip is for the hands to get "wristy" and sling the club into the back of the golf ball. Rather, the hands should lead the club into impact just as they do in a full swing, with the shaft and left forearm properly aligned at the point of contact (below, center).

Although the hands control the chip motion, it's imperative that you allow your body to rotate with the club as you hit through the ball (below, right). If you don't open up to the target through impact, the club will come into the ball on an ascending path. Ouch. Even in a short swing such as this, your entire body must work in harmony.

Of course, you'll need ample practice time to judge just how long a stroke to make in order to chip the ball different distances. Take care, however, to keep your rhythm and tempo constant. At times, you'll need to take the club back only a foot or so to produce the entire distance. Other times, you may have to swing the club nearly waist-high. Regardless of the length of your shot, your follow-through should always be longer than your backswing. Extending the follow-through forces you to accelerate through the shot. I'm sure you've heard words like *duff* or *chili-dip*. Those descriptions apply to golfers who don't accelerate on their chips.

When chipping, avoid these two common flaws and you'll be well on your way to a great up and down. One: restrict your backswing. The chip shot requires a short backstroke. When you get to the point where you must take your hands past your right knee (as in left photo), move to a less-lofted club and shorten the stroke. Two: don't ease into the ball (as in photo on right). Although the swing is short, it's still a swing and demands acceleration. If you stop at the ball, you're likely to hit the ball fat. Make a fairly long follow-through (at least longer than your backswing).

SOME GOOD ADVICE: HIT DOWN AND THROUGH

In a regular, full swing, the speed at which the club moves negates the danger of the club stopping or slowing when it hits the turf. During a chip, however, the club's involvement with the ground must be considered because the club moves at such a slow rate of speed. Poor contact, especially when the club makes contact with the ground before it strikes the golf ball, can have disastrous consequences.

The key is to hit down and through. You don't need to take any sort of divot whatsoever with a chip, but it's still very important that you strike the ball with a slightly descending

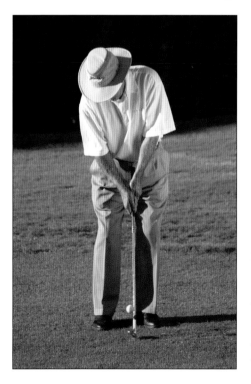

blow. That's where that audible click comes from on a well-executed pitch shot.

If you can never produce that "click" when chipping, you're probably playing the ball too far forward in your stance. On all chips, position the ball so that it rests just before the bottom part of your stroke. You can find the bottom part of your stroke by simply brushing the grass. Assume your standard chipping setup and move the club back and forth in a continuous chipping motion. As you do this, check the ground and take note where the clubhead brushes against the turf in relation to your stance. This is where you need to position the ball to ensure clean contact.

IF I ASKED YOU TO HIT A 25-YARD CHIP RIGHT NOW, could you do it? I'm not challenging your skill or technique here, but whether or not you know what 25 yards looks like. You'd be surprised how many golfers—even tour players—can't correctly judge shot lengths. Today's golfers are very flagstick oriented, and they rely too much on GPS devices and whatnot to give them their distances. I played a lot of football in my day, so I know how far 20, 30, and 45 yards is. More important, I know what these distances look like. So should you, otherwise you'll never become an expert at hitting to specific targets. Get in the practice of walking off all of your short-yardage attempts, even on the range. You'll be surprised at how quickly your eyes will learn.

SOME GOOD ADVICE: BRICK YOUR CHIPS

The most important thing you can do to improve your chipping game is to know your distances precisely. Here's a drill that can help. Find an area where you can pace off 30, 60, and 90 yards. Then place a small builder's brick at each distance. Hit pitch shots at the 30-yard brick until you land one on it. You'll get a great thrill from seeing the ball bounce way up in the air, and you should start to develop confidence and an aggressive attitude when you begin to hit such a small target with regularity. After you hit the brick from 30 yards, go for 60 then 90 yards.

LESSON 3: MAKE A PITCH FOR SUCCESS

All good shot-making starts with your eyes, because you have to see what the golf course is willing to give you. The 30-, 60-, and 90-yard pitch shots

all involve the same golf swing, but the way you approach them is a little different.

With the shorter distances, get the ball on the ground as soon as possible. Use all the green you can. Don't use a lob shot for all of your greenside approaches. A shot rolling toward the hole is a shot with a chance to go in.

As you visualize the shot and consider club selection, don't limit yourself to your sand wedge. Sometimes you'll have a better chance of getting it close if you drop down to a pitching wedge or even a 9 iron. You want to use the club that will work best for the conditions. If you're playing into a strong headwind and the pin is set back on the green, a 9 iron may be just what you need to get it close. Likewise, with a strong wind at your back, you'll want to choose a less-lofted club for a low shot that won't sail on you.

As you can guess, you've got to set up properly in order for your club and hands to work together

50-YEAR TIP: "SHOOT FOR THE TOP"

WITH SHOTS OF 75 TO 90 YARDS, THE MOST important thing is to stay aggressive. Otherwise, you'll end up short. I know hundreds of golfers who would have been great if all the pins were cut up front. On longer pitch shots, aim for the top of the pin—the flag. Your mind-set will be to go for it, and that's what you need to do with your pitches.

in a simple, consistent stroke. There's not much body movement in a good pitching swing, so the setup should put the hands in control. Start by standing tall, fairly close to the ball. If you measure from your elbow to your fingertips, you'll find that it's about 18 inches. That's about how far you want to stand from the ball. I like to stand even closer, but you should never be farther away than 18 inches.

Remember that when you stand tall, your hands will be high, setting the club in an upright position. This enhances the "feel" of your hands and fingers and quiets your body. Your head should be slightly behind the ball, raising your left shoulder so that you've set your body lines like an airplane coming in for a landing. Play the ball in the middle of your stance.

Your alignment should be square to the clubface. Remember, the clubface is going to control the trajectory and direction of the shot. So, although many golfers open up the face of their wedge, I prefer to keep it square when I can or even hood it a little bit. As you align to the target, use the entire leading edge of the clubface. (If you align using just the sweet spot of the wedge, you'll almost always be open to the target line and have to compensate somewhere during the stroke, losing consistency.) Of course, there are times when you need to hit it higher. Open the face of your wedge and open your body so that you'll swing across the target line. That's the only adjustment you'll have to make.

The swing itself is a smooth, compact motion. Break your wrists early to set the club and give your hands control of the swing. Determine the distance of the shot by the length of the backswing. For 30-yard shots, take the club back to knee-high, and then hit down and through the ball. For 60 yards, take it back to hip-high. Ninety yards? Go to waist-high. You should almost never need to swing the club higher than that.

SOME GOOD ADVICE: ALTER YOUR APPROACH

The most common chipping and pitching problem I see is that people make it too complicated. Familiarize yourself with how the ball reacts from different lies and slopes. You don't have to make major swing adjustments—you simply have to learn to recognize the patterns. And once you have the patterns down, it boils down to making just a few setup changes.

LOTS OF GREEN = PLAY IT BACK

If you have lots of green between you and the flag, use it to your advantage. A ball rolling on the ground is always easier to control than one that gets up into the air. To ensure a lower trajectory with all of your wedges, play the ball back in your stance, hood the club, or both.

LESS GREEN = OPEN IT UP

When you're faced with just a small amount of green between you and the flag, you'll need some extra height to get the ball close. All other things being equal, the easiest way to add loft is to rotate the face open at address. After you rotate the face open, don't change your grip. If I had a dollar for every time a student opened the face then regripped the club just prior to making his or her swing and returned the face back to neutral, I'd be a very rich man.

IN THE ROUGH = FIRM IT UP

When you miss a green, your ball will usually come to rest in some deep grass either to the side or long of the green. Thankfully, we don't play in U.S. Open–style conditions every day, so the typical deep-grass greenside lie won't require a chop shot or blast. What's normally required is a crisp, controlled pop on the ball via a slow, smooth swing.

Set up for the shot exactly how you'd set up to hit from a deep bunker, that is, with an open stance, with the face of your wedge slightly open, with a choked-down grip, and with the ball played forward and close to your body. Most important, firm up your grip—you don't want the long grass to twist and turn the face through impact.

The true key on the deep-grass chip is to hit down and through. The clubhead still should be traveling on a descending arc as it strikes the golf ball. When contact is made, don't stop your swing, but don't continue to a full finish, either. On these delicate blasts, it's okay to stop your swing post impact, when the shaft and your

lead arm once again form a straight line. By doing so, you'll put an extra bit of spin on the ball to better control it when it lands on the green.

I like to play these shots where the ball lands three-quarters of the way to the hole, takes a jump, and then spins to a stop with a slight trickle forward to the cup. Bumping and running can be used here, too, but in my opinion, trying to run the ball all the way to the cup will keep the golfer from hitting cleanly down on the ball, which is paramount to success.

SOME GOOD ADVICE: PRACTICE ONE-HANDED

Like anything else, you need to start your short-game practice sessions with a warm-up routine that sets the tone. The best approach I've found is to begin with the one-hand drill.

Take your sand wedge and, using just your right hand, grip it about halfway down the handle. Make a few short swings to get the tempo right. Keep your right elbow close to your side as you swing back (top photo), and extend the right arm as you swing through to the target (bottom photo). Imagine that you're reaching out to shake hands with a friend. Your arm will naturally extend as you swing through the impact area, and your right shoulder will keep working through toward the target. Now hit a few 15- or 20-yard shots using only your right hand. This allows the weight of the clubhead to dictate the stroke; the body moves only in response to the clubhead. Concentrate on hitting the ball squarely.

LESSON 4: SAND PLAY MADE EASY

Golf can fool you sometimes, especially when playing sand shots. In everything else you do, the sand means a good time—relaxing on the beach, seeing your kids play in the sandbox. But sand in a bunker strikes fear in the hearts of most golfers. Why? Tour pros thrive in bunkers, almost always giving themselves good up-and-down opportunities. Many will play their second shot on a par-5 toward a trap, figuring they have a better shot at birdie from the bunker than with a wedge from the fairway or rough.

What these players know, and what most weekend players have forgotten, is that sand can be fun. There's

no reason why you can't hit a sand shot within 10 feet of the hole at least half the time. It's the only shot in golf where you don't even have to hit the ball. So set aside your anxieties and learn to see sand as an old friend.

SOME GOOD ADVICE: "BE CREATIVE"

Don't be afraid to experiment. Once you get the hang of evaluating and understanding sand conditions and the basic sand shot, you can pick the ball, blast it, or even putt it. Just remember to accelerate through the shot and let your right shoulder swing toward the target, and you'll develop a great feel from the bunker.

When we were kids, playing in the sand was about the most fun we could ever have. Thanks to golf, some things never change.

MY BUNKER TECHNIQUE

All good sand players have one thing in common—a perfect setup position that combines the proper stance, clubface position, and dig of the feet. You'll want to stand up tall in the bunker, with your chin up and your back straight, bent from the hips, not the waist. Grip the club with your fingers and choke down a couple of inches on the grip for increased control and to lessen the chance of digging underneath the ball. Always align your feet with the clubface. For shorter shots, open the clubface and open up your stance. As the shots get longer, both the clubface and the stance should work toward square.

When it comes to digging in your feet, remember that the position of your feet will play a role in positioning the low point in your swing. In the sand, you want the low point of your swing to be just lower than the ball. For shorter shots, dig more. For longer shots, dig a little less.

Again, you'll need to practice to get the feel for how deep to position your feet, but that practice will go a long way toward helping you get the right feel for the shot. Of course, different sand conditions require different stances. Get in there and play around some.

The bunker swing itself is arms and hands. An overactive lower body can lead to skulls and fat shots and plenty of bunker misery. If you've ever sent a ball sailing over your friends' heads, you know what I mean. So stay nice and still, and swing the club back slightly to the outside. Break your left wrist early to get the club up in a V-shaped swing. Stand tall, and keep your head high throughout.

The backswing only goes to about waist-high. Keep your right elbow in close to your side for better club control. Now swing through the ball, leading with your hands and hitting the sand just behind the ball. A lot of people say you need to hit two inches behind the ball, but I say that's making things too complicated. The beauty of the sand shot is that it doesn't have to be nearly as precise as other shots. The ball will splash right out as long as you accelerate through the shot and let your right shoulder swing all the way through the ball.

Open stance, neutral shaft lean.

Hands and arms take away the club.

Quiet lower body.

"Keep your lower body quiet!"

SOME GOOD ADVICE: USE ALL OF YOUR WEDGES

As with the rest of the short game, the loft of your wedge will determine a lot about the shot you intend to hit. For short bunker shots, use your lob wedge and open the clubface. For longer shots, drop down to your sand wedge. I recommend that you carry a sand wedge with a lot of bounce. Bounce is the angle between the flange at the bottom of the club and the rear of the clubface, and it helps the clubhead respond more precisely to the sand. When the leading edge of a sand wedge hits the sand, it splashes more than it digs and helps you swing through the ball—the most important key to getting out of the bunker on the first try every time.

If you don't have a sand wedge that you absolutely love, you're already wasting strokes. It's one of the most important clubs in your bag. Remember, when Gene Sarazen invented the sand wedge back in the 1920s, it was considered as big an advantage as the long putter is today. You'd want the right shovel to dig a hole, and you want the right tool to get out of one.

"Splash" the clubhead into the sand behind the golf ball.

Post impact, continue to unwind toward target.

Lob Wedge

Sand Wedge

Some situations demand a little extra creativity. If the sand is particularly shallow, wet, or hard, use a pitching wedge instead of a sand wedge. Because the pitching wedge has less bounce than a sand wedge does, it will tend to dig a little more. Again, open the clubface for shorter shots, and move it toward square for longer ones. Now just make a normal swing and watch the ball come out prettily.

A pitching wedge will also help if you encounter a "fried egg," or buried lie, on the golf course. These lies call for a blast out of the sand. Dig in, choke down, set your hands ahead, and blast the ball out with a square clubface. Don't try to be a hero. Get the ball out—allow for plenty of roll—and then 2-putt from there.

"Just because it's a sand wedge doesn't mean it's the only club you can use in the sand."

Pitching Wedge

SOME GOOD ADVICE: BE A (GARY) PLAYER

Of all the players I've ever seen, no one can handle the bunker shot quite like Gary Player. Watch him play on television. Better yet, get out to a tournament and watch him practice his bunker shots if you get the chance. In the old days, when Player stepped into the practice bunker, he wouldn't come out until he had holed a shot, no matter how long it took. You may not need to go that far, but only by practicing in the bunkers will you begin to learn about the sand itself.

Loose, coarse sand is much different from fine-grain sand, and wet sand is another matter altogether. Some bunkers have lots of sand in them, creating a fluffy feel. Others have just a couple of inches and feel almost like hardpan underneath. Practice in as many sand conditions as you can find to get a feel for how the ball behaves. Always dig in with your feet to get a feel for the depth of the sand. Doing so will give you a head start in figuring out how the ball is going to react. The first place Player would go when he got to a tournament site was the practice bunker. By the time the weekend rolled around, the ground under his feet felt just fine. And it showed.

"How did Gary Player become the greatest bunker player of all time? He practiced!"

3

FROM THE FAIRWAY

I LOVE THE SHORT GAME, ESPECIALLY WEDGE SHOTS.

And certainly there's nothing much more rewarding in golf than busting a big drive down the middle of a fairway. But make no mistake: between your shots from the tee box and the short-game wizardry you display around the green rests the most critical part of the game—your approach from the fairway.

Iron play has always defined golf greatness. In very few instances has a tour player topped the money list with a low greens in regulation percentage. Minus the occasional chip-in, you can't make birdies if you don't hit the ball on the green with your approach shot, and that means you can never shoot a good score unless your iron swing is top notch.

I'm not going to lie to you: hitting your irons is difficult. To complicate things, there are a million ways to deliver the clubface squarely to the back of the golf ball. But all of these variations share the same simple motion, and you can boil it down to simple fundamentals. Push the club back with your left hand, and hit through it with your right hand. Over the next several pages, we'll talk a bit about wrist angles, weight shift, shoulder positioning, and whatnot, but what really matters is that you get the club moving back and through in a simple, continuous motion. Apply a few basic fundamentals, and you'll be well on your way to hitting crisp, accurate irons shots just like the pros do.

> "Iron play has always defined golf greatness. In very few instances has a tour player topped the money list with a low greens in regulation percentage."

SOME GOOD ADVICE: "YOU GOTTA HAVE BALANCE"

IN ORDER TO BE CONSISTENT WITH YOUR GOLF SWING, YOU HAVE TO STAY IN BALANCE, OTHERWISE you'll move up, down, and side-to-side, all the while destroying your swing path and plane. People naturally think they have balance, but most don't. One of the first things I do with my students is have them set up to the ball. Then I'll come in and give them a little push with my hand. You'd be surprised how easily an 80-year-old man can knock over a stronger, younger person. Balance must be built with the proper setup. The best way to achieve balance at address is to imagine you're on a basketball court, defending your goal. In so doing, you'll naturally place your feet about shoulder-width apart and bend your knees slightly. This natural "defend" position prepares you to transfer weight in any direction quickly and efficiently, exactly what a solid full swing needs. The setup may be a static position, but it's actually quite athletic. Before every swing, remember to defend!

THE FULL SWING:
IT'S ALL IN YOUR HANDS

Despite the complexity of the golf swing, iron play success begins and ends with the fingers. You can create more than 100 mph of speed with your fingers, easily the fastest parts of your body. It makes sense, then, that you should use them to your advantage when you swing a golf club. Think of the hummingbird. A hummingbird doesn't fly with its belly. It uses its wings, which can move up to an amazing 700 mph.

Of course, in order to use your hands optimally, you need to have the right grip. I've always said that the right grip is the one that feels the most comfortable. Use an interlocking, overlapping, 10-finger—whatever. The most important thing is to make sure that you grip as much of the club as you can in your fingers. You want your fingers to dominate your swing. They'll never be able to if you grip the club with your palms. Palms are good for shaking hands and giving high-fives, not for swinging a golf club.

When I say that all you have to do is swing the club with your hands, it doesn't mean you can move the clubhead all over the place and get good results. The hands have to be in the right position in order to hit decent shots. Roger Clemens uses his hands to throw a baseball, but he'd still be pitching in the Little League if he didn't use his hands correctly.

When I teach a student, I like to have him or her swing to the waist-high takeaway position. At this point in the swing, we check to make sure the hands are in the right place—specifically, that the thumbs and the clubhead point straight up at the sky. Some people feel they have to rotate their hands, or fan the club, in order to get into this critical position. You don't if you coordinate your hands and wrist hinge with the turning of the shoulders on the takeaway. Try it and you'll see what I mean.

It's important that when you take away the club with your hands, you don't move the clubhead too far to the inside of the target line. I see a lot of amateurs do this when trying to swing with their hands. The reason this happens is that these players over-turn their hips. When you take away the club, it's a good idea to keep the left hip exactly where it was at address. When you let it

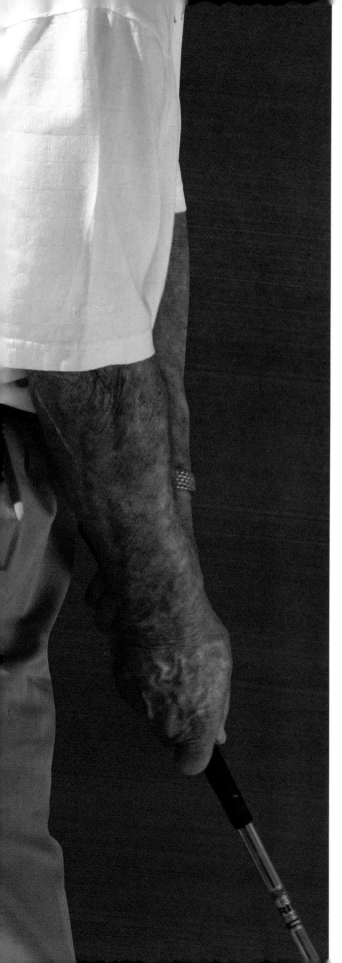

slide or turn with your shoulders, you not only lose needed tension, but you also move the club on a path that's too far to the inside, which ruins the swing as soon as it has begun.

When you take away the club, the face automatically opens to your target line. To get back to square at impact (unless you like to slice), think of where your hands need to be in the follow-through. They need to mirror the hand position in the waist-high takeaway position—that is, with the thumbs and clubhead pointing at the sky. Therefore, you need to "close the door." That's another easy thing to do. You close doors every day, so there's no reason why you can't do it with a golf club. The way to do it is to think of where you're swinging toward. I like to use the reference of a baseball diamond to explain this. You're at home plate and you have first base to your right, third base on your left, and second base in front of you. If you swing to first base, you'll push or hook the ball. If you swing to third, you'll pull or slice the ball. But if you can swing your hands toward second base, you've got something. I always ask my students to swing toward second base. If you can think of swinging to second, you'll not only generate the proper swingpath, but you'll allow your hands to "close the door" to get that clubface nice and square at impact.

WHAT MAKES A GOLF SWING GREAT?

Establishing balance at address and maintaining it throughout the swing and using a hands-dominated motion are my hallmark full-swing keys. But we all know there's a lot more going on when you swing an iron from the fairway. And while I recommend that you always favor the simplest motion possible and break down your swing thoughts to the most basic of images, it's important that you become familiar with the complex dynamics of the full swing. Because it's impossible for me to know which errors are plaguing your motion right now, I think it's a good idea to take a look at what a good golf swing looks like position by position. See if you can incorporate any of these moves into your technique. However, be wary of making things too complicated. Remember, full-swing perfection is all in your hands.

1. BALANCE

When you watch a great golfer swinging a club, the first thing that stands out is his balance. Compare that to your own motion or to one of the lesser-skilled members of your foursome, someone who's constantly falling backward, forward, away, and to the target. If all of my students swung with an attempt to maintain balance instead of killing the golf ball, they'd drop five strokes immediately. Balance throughout the swing is created by a proper setup, one that features the following ingredients: (a) head positioned behind the ball, with the right shoulder situated slightly below the left and both shoulders aligned parallel left of target; (b) neutral hands (positioned just inside the left leg) with knees slightly flexed ("stacking" the chest, knees, and toes); and (c) feet positioned slightly wider than shoulder width to provide a solid foundation.

"If there's one thing that defines a great swing, it's balance. Without it, you'll never find the positions needed to properly deliver the clubhead."

Arms are in front of the chest, and the clubshaft and left forearm are in line.

Hands bring the club skyward without any lifting or rising of the head or body.

Clubface angle and left forearm match perfectly.

Both arms remain loose, pulled from their sockets by the force of rotation.

2. A SOLID TAKEAWAY

A great takeaway features a clubhead that travels straight back along the target line with the face remaining pointed at the golf ball until the wrists hinge. This can be accomplished only by syncing the hands and shoulders. Another aspect of a good takeaway (and golf swing, in general) is that the arms remain in front of the chest. Also, notice how the knees remain flexed, with the left knee pointing at the golf ball. This helps produce a tighter coil at the top of the backswing.

3. ROTATION

If you're great at the top, your chances of success increase dramatically. Notice: (a) the shaft lies short of parallel and directly above the right shoulder; (b) the left wrist has kept from cupping, and the right forefinger supports the club; (c) the left shoulder has rotated to a point directly below the chin (the right will replace it on the downswing); (d) the right knee has willingly accepted the transfer of weight and held off the tendency to straighten; and (e) the left knee is still pointing at the golf ball.

The key to a great top position is to rotate your body behind the ball within the circle defined by your hips. It's also critical to maintain your spine angle—no lifting of the torso required. Think of keeping your left shoulder as low as possible.

4. INSIDE ARRIVAL

Impact is often referred to as "the moment of truth" in the golf swing. In my opinion, this lofty title more appropriately describes the downswing. Impact is but a natural result of what occurred on the way back down to the golf ball. If your downswing sequence is solid, your contact with the ball will be, too.

Your priority in the downswing is to keep the clubshaft on the proper plane. You'll know when you're on the correct path when the shaft sits between your forearms midway down. This places the club on the correct, power-rich, inside path to the golf ball. One key for achieving this state is to keep your left shoulder from rotating open too quickly. Your shoulders and hips (following the lead of your hands) should turn in sync and then should keep turning. Also, stay planted! Great swings feature spine angles that are rigid, knees that remain flexed, and a steady head.

Great swings ultimately end up here, ready to deliver the club to the ball from inside the target line, with the butt end of the club pointing at the golf ball and the shaft lying neatly between the two forearms. If you're not right here, you won't maximize your results.

To become a great iron player, you'll have to learn to unleash stored energy into the ball. Simply unwind, with the right shoulder rotating down the target line and under the chin. This rapid-yet-controlled uncoiling occurs without any head movement.

5. A SOLID IMPACT POSITION

Great golfers produce great contact. Here's what I look for: (a) the right side sits slightly lower than the left, which forms a wall to hit through (notice how the left shoulder, left arm, left hip, and the shaft form a straight line); (b) the hands have returned to the same position they held at address, with the left wrist as flat as it can be and both hands leading the clubhead into the ball; and (c) the right foot has transferred weight to the left without the body or head moving ahead of the ball.

"The golf swing is simple —it's simply a turn back and a turn forward. Your right knee serves as the hub for both turns."

6. NATURAL RELEASE

After you've made contact with the ball, the swing is hardly over. You must continue to unwind and get everything—hands, hips, and club—left of your target line. In the photo at right, notice how, in the release, the arms are fully extended and the right hand has rotated over the left. Great. The finish (below right) is even better, defined by extreme balance, a straight back, and even knees.

"The best swing advice I can give is to keep that right shoulder moving under your chin and your hands low through the hitting area."

SOME GOOD ADVICE: SPIN THE TOP

You've heard me say that golf is simple, but don't get me wrong: a good golf swing doesn't take shape overnight. It takes practice. Rome wasn't built in a day. It wasn't built in a month, either, but you can start grooving the right type of swing today by reverting to your childhood and spinning the top.

We've all spun tops before. Although you don't see too many of them around anymore, I'm sure you know how to make one work. Just wrap a string tightly around the top and let 'er go. It's not a hard thing to do as long as you keep the string nice and tight.

The same holds true in the golf swing. When you take the club back (wrap the string around the top), you've got to create a nice, tight package. From there, you start your hands in motion (pull the string), and let your hips spin (like the top).

Simple, right? Right. Although you'd be surprised by how few golfers can spin the top correctly. The key is to start the backswing by turning your shoulders, and keep on turning them. I always let the left-side shoulder seam on my shirt go past my left knee. When I see that it has, I know I've made a solid turn with my upper body.

A big mistake amateurs make when turning their shoulders is over-turning the hips. You have to turn against a firm left side, otherwise you won't keep the tension in your swing. It's like winding a top with a lot of slack in the string. The top's never going to spin against a loose string, and your body won't swing the club with power against a weak left side.

Make your shoulder turn, but keep your left hip right where it was at address. Do that right now, and drop your left hand on top of your left thigh. See how tight your muscles are? That's the energy you'll use to hit the ball down the fairway. You're ready to spin the top.

HOW TO SPIN THE TOP

Tightening the string is simple. Spinning the top's a bit harder. The key is to lead with your hands. It's important that you don't confuse "lead with the hands" with making an early release. This happens when you don't allow the hands to drop to start the forward swing and instead go immediately at the ball. It's like an apple falling out of a tree. It falls straight onto the ground, not

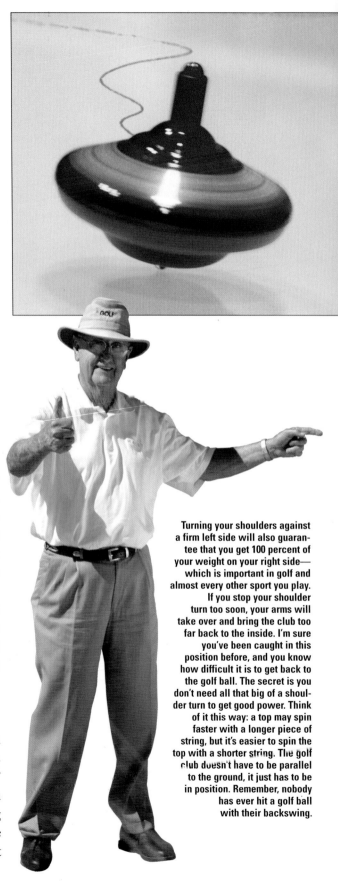

Turning your shoulders against a firm left side will also guarantee that you get 100 percent of your weight on your right side—which is important in golf and almost every other sport you play. If you stop your shoulder turn too soon, your arms will take over and bring the club too far back to the inside. I'm sure you've been caught in this position before, and you know how difficult it is to get back to the golf ball. The secret is you don't need all that big of a shoulder turn to get good power. Think of it this way: a top may spin faster with a longer piece of string, but it's easier to spin the top with a shorter string. The golf club doesn't have to be parallel to the ground, it just has to be in position. Remember, nobody has ever hit a golf ball with their backswing.

straight into your mouth. Believe me, allowing the hands to drop on the downswing is the hardest thing to do in golf. I started teaching my son this move as soon as he was able to hold a golf club, and he finally got it down when he was 15 years old.

There are two things that will help you drop your hands (or find the slot, make the magic move, etc.) like you're supposed to:

1) Think of wearing your right pocket out with the back of your right hand on the downswing. It's a good visual, and it's worked for me.

2) Make sure you're in the right position at the top, specifically, that your right elbow points toward the ground. Keeping the elbow pointed downward (not fllying out) will not only make dropping the hands a more natural move, but also will keep your swing more on-plane and prevent coming over the top.

Although it's a simple move, I find that a lot of players, high-handicappers especially, don't keep the right elbow tucked on the backswing. They allow it to fly or pin it behind their right shoulder. Not only does this put the club—and golfer—in a poor position at the top, but it makes dropping the hands correctly to start the downswing more difficult than it has to be. If you keep that elbow tucked as you swing to the top, your hands will be on-plane and ready to drop and move the club on that inside-out, power-rich swingpath. It will also keep you from stopping your shoulder turn too soon and moving the club to the top with too much arm action.

If you have trouble keeping the right elbow tight against your right side, use the following drill. Grab a towel and tuck it into your right armpit. Then simply make your swing. The object of the drill is to keep that towel in place through impact. The only way you can do this is to keep the right elbow tucked during the backswing and to let your hands drop straight down to start the downswing. If you let your right elbow fly or swing to the top with just your hands, then the towel will drop.

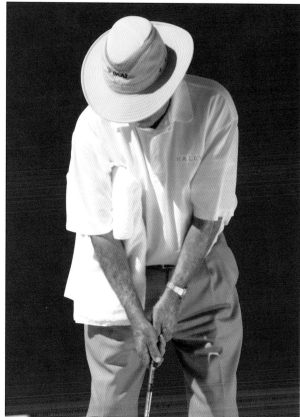

Guarantee a proper shoulder turn by swinging with a towel tucked in your right armpit.

Don't worry if you have trouble dropping the hands—this move takes practice. But it's an important component of a sound golf swing. If you don't drop your hands, you'll end up leading the club with your shoulders, which will power the ball anywhere but where you want it to go. At the very least, keep the elbow tucked and then pointed at the ground at the top.

In the end, keep things simple. You had fun as a kid spinning the top. You can have fun hitting a golf ball if you do the same.

If the towel drops at the top position (above left), you've stopped your shoulders too soon and allowed your right elbow to fly. The above right photo shows the proper shoulder turn.

PUTTING IT ALL TOGETHER: ADD THE KEY INGREDIENT

The golf swing's a funny thing. Sometimes it's racked with errors, yet somehow, at impact, everything is where it needs to be and the ball shoots off powerfully in the direction you intended. Other times, every shift, angle, and hinge is perfect, yet a small misstep on the way to the ball results in shots that can only be described as horrific. In the first instance, Lady Luck is certainly on your side, but as we all know, she rarely hangs around for too long. And the fact that a single hiccup can bring your whole technique crashing down is, to put it bluntly, just the way golf is.

One of the most damaging errors I've seen consistently throughout this period of time is knee movement, specifically a straightening of the right knee on the backswing. This seemingly innocent mistake gives the golfer almost zero chance of making a quality pass at the ball and fuels both flawed backswings and downswings. As you'll soon learn, however, correctly managing right-knee movement makes producing a

> "Watch any accomplished golfer, and you'll see him or her retain right knee flex throughout the backswing and beyond. It's an athletic positioning that fuels both power and control."

fundamentally sound motion a fairly easy task. Truly, it's the key ingredient to any good swing.

By properly retaining flex in the right knee, I create a stable platform to support a large shoulder turn and constricted lower-body turn. Keeping the flex on the downswing also allows me to use the ground for leverage to swing powerfully through impact.

Here, I've lost my hub, and not only has my lower body turned too far, but my weight shifted first to the outside of my right foot and, with nothing to support it, beyond my right hip. From here, I can only make a weak slap at the ball, a move devoid of leverage and power.

side the right leg. Also, the flexed right knee affords the stability needed to transfer weight to the right side on the backswing and position it in the right hip at the top. Furthermore, the flexed-knee position keeps the clubshaft on the appropriate backswing plane, established by the arrangement of the arms and club at address.

If and when the right-knee flex is lost, as is the case with so many amateur swings, weight is thrown from the right side back to the left (reverse pivot). That's a big no-no. Second, straightening the knee moves the backswing plane to the inside, which can lead to all kinds of downswing misery. Third, losing the right-knee flex gives your lower body too much room to turn and allows it to sway away from the ball on the backswing. As a result, all of the coil is lost. Potential energy is nil, and all you're left with power-wise is what you can generate by moving your arms as fast as you can back down to the ball. It's an unleveraged motion that's both weak and inconsistent and certainly no part of a successful swing.

From the top, things can only get worse. With a straight right knee, the only way you can get back to the ball is to slide violently targetward, a flaw devoid of rotation and, more often than not, one from which most amateurs cannot recover. Second, as the club moves down, your inability to push off from a straight right leg will strand weight on the right side at impact. Expect weak, glancing blows and numerous topped shots. The strong, athletic properties that define a fundamentally sound golf swing are lost. Amazing what a single flaw can do, right?

A flexed right knee throughout the backswing facilitates coil, the needed separation between the upper and lower body that creates potential energy that's eventually released into the back of the golf ball. A flexed right knee braces the lower body, stopping its turn while allowing the upper body to perform its full rotation and, most important, keeps the right hip from moving out-

To properly maintain right-knee flex throughout the swing, I advocate presetting the flex at address by slightly kicking in the right knee toward the target. The tension created by this preset fuels a strong backswing coil, keeps the club on plane, and allows me to use the ground for leverage to push off and explode through the hitting zone. You can do this with a standard knee position at address (as in photo at right), but it's not as easy as when you use the preset.

All good, full swings begin with weight favoring the right side at address, not the left.

positioning at setup. Too many amateurs begin with not enough knee flex and too much bend from the waist. The proper posture at address is one that's athletic, or ready for action. From your static position at address, you should feel as if you could move in any direction without hesitation, like a linebacker in football ready to pounce toward all sides of the field.

As far as maintaining flex, I advise my students to preset a solid bent right knee. This preset goes beyond simply flexing the knee and holding it there. At address, and without lifting your right foot, bend in your right knee slightly, as if you're trying to point your kneecap at the golf ball. It's just a slight kick in to the left. You should feel some tension in your right knee and sense some tension running up your right quadriceps and through your right hip. That bit of tension in your right knee and hip will both limit your lower-body rotation (thus increasing coil) and stabilize your backswing. At the top, the tension created at address by kicking in the right knee still should reside in your right side. Use that tension to shift your weight through to your left as you bring the club into impact and beyond.

Properly using the right knee as a rotational hub and as a support to accept the backswing weight shift to the right side is as easy as, well, maintaining flex in that knee until the swing unwinds through impact. Sounds easy enough, yet you'd be surprised how difficult it is for some players to retain flex. One reason for this is poor

Use of this technique has allowed many of my students to better sense the physics of weight shift. It demystifies the swing, making it as simple as moving the club to the top and then back to the ball. There are many ways to turn a good swing into a bad one. So, too, are there many methods to make a bad swing decent. Presetting the right knee is just one of those techniques.

THE BEST IRON SWING I'VE EVER SEEN

AS YOU CAN GUESS, I'VE SEEN A MILLION swings in my life and probably swung a club myself at least another million times. To me, the full swing is a piece of art, but with the added dimensions of sound and feel. There's nothing quite like hearing the click of a crisply struck iron shot then watching the ball race out and up before falling gently on the ground. If you ever get the chance, go to an early round of a tour event and take a seat near the practice area. Like me, you'll become almost hypnotized by the rhythmic sensation of a purely swung iron. When I'm on tour, the range is where all the excitement is, and even after a 30-year teaching career on the professional circuits, I still get a kick out of watching those boys knock down the range flags.

I had the privilege of working with a lot of the original players of the Senior PGA Tour, which took root in the mid-1980s. I was with Chi Chi Rodriguez a lot back then, but I also had time to work with one of golf's most unique players: Dave Hill. Older readers will remember Hill, who won 13 PGA Tour events and played in three Ryder Cups. But despite his success, Hill is most often pegged as a fiery pro who often did more damage with his tongue than with his golf equipment. The stories of him threatening Bernard Gallacher at the 1969 Ryder Cup and his remarks about Hazeltine Golf Club at the 1970 U.S. Open (in which he finished runner-up to Tony Jacklin), describing it as "80 acres of corn and a few animals short of a farm pasture") have surely made him somewhat infamous. But to those deeply involved in golf, Hill is credited with carrying the U.S. Ryder Cup team on his back in 1969, 1971, and 1973 and, in my opinion, owner of the best iron swing I've ever seen.

How good was Hill's swing? I could go on for pages, but at least know this: he won the 1969 Vardon Trophy (awarded for lowest scoring average on tour), which was a remarkable feat considering that his playing peers Jack Nicklaus, Arnold Palmer, Lee Trevino, and Gary Player were basically in their prime. He was a true student of the swing and fretted over mechanics like a jeweler does over a diamond under a microscope.

What Hill perfected, and what most recreational iron swings lack, is setting the club at the top. He was always—and I mean always—absolutely perfect at the top. More important, he had patience. He'd set the club and wait for the perfect moment to drop it into the slot and sling it toward the golf ball. Even some of today's leading professionals lose it a little. But Hill never lost control of the club and, for an average-sized guy, hit some of the most powerful irons this side of Nick Price.

Learn from Hill's technique. After you bring the club to the top, remain in control. A lot of weekend players are guilty of letting the club drop toward the head via an elbow or wrist bend before initiating the downswing. Have patience! Move through your transition without allowing the club to droop. If you do, you'll always start out on plane and give yourself the best possible chance of crisp, pure contact.

A very important swing key is to set the club at the top and remain in control of it throughout the transition (left).
If you allow it to drop (right), your chances of success dwindle.

SWING THOUGHTS THAT REALLY WORK

It never hurts to associate swing needs with some more recognizable tasks. I'm sure you've used swing thoughts before, and I encourage you to continue the practice. Swing thoughts have the uncanny ability to demystify the swing instantly, and as I've said before, anything that can simplify the golf swing is a good thing. Following are a few swing thoughts that I use and teach that, for me, have worked for the better part of 70 years.

1. POINT YOUR THUMBS

The takeaway is a section of the swing in which many errors easily can creep into your technique and wreak havoc on your results. The basic requirement of the takeaway is to establish the proper plane while moving the club skyward and slightly around your body, all the while keeping the face in the proper position and making sure it doesn't unduly close or fly open. How do you make simple work of this dizzying array of commands? Simply point your thumbs. Here's how it works.

Without a club, swing your arms back as you do on your takeaway and stop them at waist high. Now look and see where your thumbs point. They should be pointing directly skyward. If they point behind you, you've swung too far to the inside or over-rotated your arms, opening the face (both of which are very common errors). As you swing through to the waist-high release position, again check your thumbs. Just as in the backswing, they should point toward the sky. Think "thumbs up to thumbs up," and you'll be just fine.

Back and Ready

Forward and Foiled

2. THROW A PASS

Ever watch a football game on TV and hear the commentator make the remark (usually after a poor performance by the quarterback), "he's throwing off his front foot"? It's a common criticism that, in my opinion, holds a lot of weight. In any athletic maneuver, whether it's hitting a baseball, shooting a free throw, or throwing a football, you have to push off your rear foot.

Watch Peyton Manning throw a pass. He drops back into the pocket, brings the football up, and sets his weight over his back leg. From there, he throws with his hand, using his rear foot to push off the ground and add power to his toss.

Same goes for the golf swing—you have to be on your right side at the top in order to swing the club with any kind of power. Swinging a golf club from the front foot makes about as much sense as throwing a football from your front foot. You'll get zero leverage from your front side. Get back, stay back, and throw a touchdown.

3. SLAP YOURSELF

Whereas the football image works well for your downswing, "giving yourself a slap" will work wonders for your setup. As I've mentioned numerous times, it's important to create a shift of weight to the right side in

the backswing, and it's a good idea to jumpstart the process by presetting your weight at address. When I feel myself getting ahead of the ball, I take my address then give myself a fake slap across my left cheek (photo at right). This reminds me to move more toward my right side at the setup and keep my head behind the ball until my head is pulled up into the finish (photo below).

Are you part of the living dead (as in this photo), or ready for Sunday dinner (as in the photo on the right)?

4. AVOID RIGOR MORTIS

We all know what rigor mortis is and that it applies only to the deceased. That being said, it's amazing how many dead golfers I see on the tee box. Whether it's nerves or fear, a lot of recreational players I teach get so tensed up at address that it looks as if they'd be more comfortable in a casket than a golf cart. You need to be relaxed to make an athletic setup and swing.

If you ever feel rigor mortis creeping into your swing, take a few moments during your preshot routine to inhale and exhale deeply a few times and shake your hands out a bit. As you set up to the ball, remember your dinner manners. Do you slouch over the Sunday table with your head turned down, away from all your family and friends? Of course not! Instead, you sit straight up and look at the other people at the table. That's the way I want you to address a golf ball. When your spine is straight, you can easily turn your shoulders around it, and by keeping your head up, your left shoulder can easily turn under your chin, just as it should. Remember, a normal head weighs approximately 14 pounds. That's a lot of weight to be hanging off your spin. It can—and will—get in the way.

DRIVE TIME

4

TO ME, PLAYING GOLF IS LIKE PAINTING A PICTURE.

It takes all kinds of brush strokes to complete the picture—long, colorful ones and short ones placed just right. It's the same way on the golf course—the strokes make driving the golf ball so important. When you stand on the tee box and look down that long fairway, you're staring at a blank canvas. The drive is the first—and boldest—stroke you're going to apply to the hole. After that stoke is made, you simply fill in the rest.

In my long association with the game of golf, I've seen every type of drive possible, from the boring mammoth blasts showcased on the professional tours to the pop-ups, flares, and banana balls common among the recreational ranks. The main differences between a great drive and a groaner are found in technique and—surprisingly—attitude. Whereas a skilled player views the driver as a weapon, less-accomplished golfers tend to approach driving with fear or, at the very least, doubt. Over the next several pages, I'm going to help you with your technique with a step-by-step guide to swinging the driver correctly. From setup to finish and with a few notes on tempo and timing, you'll have what you'll need to perfect your performance on the tee box.

Now, as far as your confidence goes, do what every good driver of the ball—even a pro—does: aim away from trouble. Sounds simple, but you'd be surprised, even at yourself, how often golfers simply take the middle route when planning where to drive the ball in the fairway. The key is to give yourself as wide a safety margin as you can. If there's water on the right side of the hole, tee up your ball on the right side of the tee box and aim up the left side of the fairway. If your ensuing drive flies straight, you're in perfect shape. If it slices, you'll probably be in an even better position, and if it goes left—well, at least your ball isn't in the water. See what I mean?

On every drive, plan your strategy from behind the ball, and pick out an easily recognizable target. Don't look for a patch of grass on the fairway or the edge of a bunker. Instead, look to the sky. Find a nice puffy cloud with which to align your shot, or the top of a tree down the fairway. I like to use above-ground references because it seems to get me focused on hitting the ball on a nice, high trajectory. Plus, you'll swing a bit easier because you've eliminated the pressure of having to hit an exact spot in the fairway.

Okay, let's get that painting started.

SOME GOOD ADVICE: FOCUS ON THE RIGHT FOOT

There are many keys to driving the ball well, but above all else, strive to have your body and head behind the ball at the point of contact. The moment your body and/or head gets ahead of the ball (moves toward the target), you're toast. And while a golfer should never confuse staying behind the ball with not making a forward weight shift, the importance of hitting off the right side can never be stressed enough. If you've made a proper driver swing, you should be able to see your right foot free and clear as you make contact with the golf ball. At address, focus on the right foot instead of the golf ball (don't worry, it's not going anywhere), and keep your eyes there until the momentum of your swing pulls your head up into the finish.

DRIVER SWING PRIMER

The secret to good driving is all around you. Watch how someone sweeps with a broom. Do they make long, jerky motions? No. They execute a simple motion with the hands controlling and the body simply helping out. Maybe the best thing you can do is take a kid to the playground and go to the swing set. As you push the swing chair, what do you do? You balance yourself and make an unhurried, rhythmic push, subconsciously staying back and releasing with your hands and arms. The result is a smooth but powerful stroke. The key is to re-create that feeling on the tee box. The following tips should help.

I F YOU WANT TO HIT WITH POWER, IT'S important that you become familiar with one of the most critical components of vigorous driving: weight shift. Unleashing as much energy as possible into the golf ball begins with storing as much energy as possible on the backswing. Gathering energy for the backswing starts with transferring weight to your right side as you take the club to the top and ends with moving that weight to your front side on the downswing. Jumpstart the process by situating the majority of your weight on your back foot at the setup—there's nothing wrong with cheating. You know you're solid if, at the top, you can raise your front foot without losing your balance.

THE SETUP

The key to a good golf swing—and this is especially true with the driver—is a good setup. You'll never be consistent without mastering the fundamentals of the setup. Furthermore, if and when your driver goes haywire, you'll need to go back to fundamentals in order to get your long game back on track.

All good drivers are balanced over the golf ball. If you don't have balance in the beginning, you won't have it at the top, in the downswing—wherever. So start by positioning your feet slightly outside your shoulders and by placing your weight on the balls of your feet. Stand tall, with your left shoulder higher than the right (about the same distance as your left hand sits higher than your right on the grip). I tell my students that you need to copy an airplane coming in for a landing, which means you must tilt your spin slightly away from the target and situate your right shoulder lower than your left. This way, you'll be able to sweep the clubhead up and through the hitting area. (Remember, you're driving the ball—no divots necessary!) Keep your head high and not buried in your chest. Keeping your head down will only create another obstacle to swing through on the way back down to the golf ball.

1. **HEAD UP, EYES FOCUSED BEHIND THE BALL TO KEEP THE BODY FROM CREEPING FORWARD.**

2. **LEFT SHOULDER SITUATED HIGHER THAN THE RIGHT SHOULDER, VIA A SPINE TILT AWAY FROM THE TARGET (POINT YOUR SHIRT BUTTONS AT THE GOLF BALL AS A GUIDE).**

3. **BEND TOWARD THE BALL FROM THE HIPS, NOT THE WAIST (A BIG DIFFERENCE).**

4. **LEFT KNEE RELAXED AND BENT (IT SHOULD NEVER STRAIGHTEN UNTIL POST IMPACT).**

5. **BALL PLAYED TOWARD THE FRONT FOOT. USE THE LOGO ON YOUR SHIRT AS A GUIDE.**

6. **FEET OUTSIDE THE SHOULDERS AND WEIGHT ON THE BALLS OF YOUR FEET FOR BALANCE.**

W HEN TAKING AWAY THE CLUB, ALWAYS THINK "LOW AND SLOW." FAR TOO MANY AMATEURS make the mistake of hinging the wrists too early in the backswing (photo at left). Instead, keep the club moving straight back as far as you can until you feel the natural tendency of the wrists to hinge (photo at right).

THE TAKEAWAY

On the takeaway, most people tend to overturn in a search for more power. Overturning, however, will rob you of everything you're trying to gain with the driver. The truth is, it's your hands and fingers that generate clubhead speed. You can't belly-whip the ball. As you take away the club, keep it low to the ground. Then let the wrists cock. You should also make a natural shift of weight from the balls of both feet toward the right heel, all the while maintaining the spine angle and bend you established at the address.

1. LEAD SHOULDER MOVING AWAY FROM THE TARGET AND UNDER THE CHIN, NOT INTO IT.

2. SPINE ANGLE MAINTAINED—DIPPING OR LIFTING NEED NOT APPLY.

3. HANDS MOVE THE CLUB STRAIGHT BACK WITHOUT ANY BOWING OR CUPPING.

4. CLUBFACE STILL POINTS DIRECTLY AT THE GOLF BALL. IMAGINE A LIGHT EMANATING FROM THE FACE AND SHINING ON THE GOLF BALL. BE WARY OF ROLLING YOUR HANDS AND POINTING THE CLUBFACE TOO MUCH TOWARD THE SKY.

5. WEIGHT SHIFTING TOWARD THE RIGHT HEEL— EXACTLY WHERE IT SHOULD BE.

THERE ARE TWO PARTS OF A SUCCESSFUL BACKSWING: AN AROUND PART AND AN UP-AND-down-down part. Most golfers can get the up-and-down-down part—that's a matter of simply lifting and dropping your hands and arms. The trouble usually stems from the around requirement. How does one turn? One way to demystify this task is to focus on the left shoulder. On the backswing, focus on turning the left shoulder under (left) and not into (right) your chin. On the downswing, the process repeats itself, this time with the right shoulder as the hands move the club into the impact zone.

AT THE TOP

The top of the backswing is a very nebulous state of affairs, existing for only a split second between the end of the backswing and the start of the downswing. Nonetheless, its importance is far reaching and holds serious sway for what happens next in the swing. Basically, the most important facet of the backswing is control. If you're set and solid and own the following needs of the top position, half the battle is won.

1. DRIVER SHORT OF PARALLEL—YOU DON'T NEED TO MIMIC JOHN DALY FOR DECENT YARDS.

2. HANDS AS FAR AWAY FROM THE HEAD AS POSSIBLE—A GREAT AND EASY SWING THOUGHT FOR THE DISTANCE-CHALLENGED PLAYER.

3. SHOULDERS TURNED A FULL 90 DEGREES, MOVING CORRECTLY UNDER THE CHIN AND IN A POWER-PACKED POSITION.

4. YES, THE SPINE ANGLE HAS BEEN MAINTAINED.

5. THE HIPS HAVE TURNED, SURELY, BUT ONLY ABOUT HALF AS MUCH AS THE SHOULDERS. IT'S THE DIFFERENTIAL BETWEEN SHOULDER AND HIP TURN THAT CREATES COIL—THE POTENTIAL ENERGY THAT WILL BE UNLEASHED INTO THE GOLF BALL ON THE DOWNSWING.

6. RIGHT KNEE FLEXED AND SERVING AS THE HUB AROUND WHICH THE UPPER BODY TURNS.

7. THE BACK FOOT IS FIRMLY PLANTED AND IN POSITION TO ACCEPT THE MAJORITY OF WEIGHT AS IT SHIFTS TO THE RIGHT SIDE.

THE DOWNSWING

From the top of the swing, think about making a nice, smooth transition. Too many players jerk their right shoulders and try to hit the ball with the arms from the top. That's a recipe for the dreaded over-the-top move (slice). Instead, think about making a throw to second base (with third base being left of target and first base to the far right of target). Don't think about first or third. Just let it go, and try to get that runner trying to steal second.

1. DESPITE THE TREMENDOUS FORCES MOVING FORWARD, THE HEAD REMAINS BEHIND THE BALL.

2. THE UPPER BODY BEGINS TO UNCOIL WITHOUT MOVING TOWARD THE TARGET.

3. THE RIGHT WRIST RETAINS ITS HINGE. IT'S VERY IMPORTANT TO RETAIN RIGHT WRIST COCK AS LONG AS POSSIBLE INTO THE DOWNSWING.

4. THE FORWARD LEG BEGINS TO STRAIGHTEN, PREPARING ITSELF TO SERVE AS A POST THROUGH WHICH THE CLUBHEAD WILL SLING INTO THE RELEASE.

5. WEIGHT MOVES FROM THE RIGHT HEEL TOWARD THE TOES ON YOUR LEFT FOOT, FACILITATING THE PROPER, FORWARD TRANSFER OF WEIGHT.

"Think about making a throw to second base (with third base being left of target and first base to the far right of target). Let it go, and try to get that runner trying to steal second."

I F YOU HANG AROUND ME LONG ENOUGH, YOU MIGHT JUST TELL ME TO KEEP MY TRAP SHUT WHEN I mention "down and through" too many times. It's one of my favorite sayings, as every great golf swing maneuvers the clubhead down and through the golf ball, creating a perfect divot—unless you're swinging the driver. When you have a driver in your hands, it's important that you swing "up and through," with the clubhead ascending through the hitting area. This helps maximize power and makes full use of the loft and sweet-spot capabilities of your driver. The key to swinging on an ascending arc through the hitting zone is to stay behind the ball and to come into impact with the right shoulder moving under the chin, yet toward the target. Ascend through impact, get that ball flying high into the air, and watch those yards pile up.

IMPACT

Impact. Contact. The moment of truth. We all have words to describe the millisecond during which the clubface and the golf ball are as one. In teaching circles, many arguments have been waged whether the proper impact position can be taught. In my opinion, it can't, but that doesn't mean you can't at least be aware of what a solid impact position looks like. If you know what should be happening, you'll just be that much more cognizant of performing the moves that can at least help you arrive at a solid contact state. What I tell all of my students is that if you focus on maintaining balance, a lot of these moves take care of themselves.

1. I CAN'T STRESS THIS ENOUGH—HEAD IS STILL BEHIND THE BALL (BUT TURNING TOWARD THE TARGET).

2. SHIRT BUTTONS POINT TOWARD THE GOLF BALL, JUST LIKE AT ADDRESS.

3. HIPS UNWIND WITHOUT SLIDING TOWARD THE TARGET.

4. EVEN THIS LATE IN THE DOWNSWING, THE RIGHT WRIST IS STILL HINGED, READY TO DELIVER ANOTHER LAYER OF ENERGY INTO THE GOLF BALL.

5. THAT'S RIGHT—THE RIGHT KNEE IS STILL FLEXED.

I VE PLAYED GOLF WITH A LOT OF GREAT STICKS in my day, and to a man, no one could hit the ball farther than my lifelong friend, New York Yankees Hall of Famer Mickey Mantle. Mickey could out-drive everyone, tour player or otherwise. Remember the 2001 U.S. Open with the 352-yard 17th at Southern Hills Country Club in Tulsa, Oklahoma? Mickey needed only two clubs on that hole during our regular matches there: a driver and a putter. On the Herculean 454-yard 1st hole at Southern Hills, Mickey often hit a sand wedge for his second shot—long before the days of titanium drivers, graphite shafts, and multilayer golf balls. How did he do it? Well, in both golf and baseball, Mickey made a point of hitting from his right side (or left side if he was batting left-handed). In other words, he hung back on his rear hip until the last possible moment, thereby unleashing as much strength and speed as possible into the golf ball.

Be like Mickey—hang back, then let 'er rip.

THE RELEASE

Can you make a release, or does it just happen? Swing pundits have fretted over this question for ages, but I'm one to believe that you can—and should—be in conscious control of the release position. After all, much of it depends on the position of your hands, and you certainly can control your hands more than any other part of your body. Without getting too technical, the most important thing to focus on post impact is a firm left side. Your left hip and leg should form a straight line. That creates the wall for your clubhead to crash through to power the ball down the fairway. If your left hip is outside the left leg, you've swung with too much leg slide and not enough turn.

1. A PROPER RELEASE ALWAYS DISPLAYS ARMS THAT ARE FULLY EXTENDED AND CROSSED OVER ONE ANOTHER. FULL EXTENSION IS A MUST FOR ACCURACY AND POWER.

2. THE FINGERS IN THE LEFT HAND ARE STILL VISIBLE. THIS INDICATES THAT THE CLUBHEAD WAS SQUARE TO THE TARGET LINE THROUGH IMPACT.

3. THE LEFT HIP AND LEG ARE STILL IN LINE AND STRAIGHT. THIS POSITION IS ABSOLUTELY NECESSARY IF YOU WANT TO STRIKE THE BALL WITH AUTHORITY. A FIRM LEFT SIDE ALSO HELPS THE CLUBHEAD GAIN SPEED THROUGH THE IMPACT ZONE.

4. THE RIGHT FOOT LIFTS NOT BY CONSCIOUS EFFORT, BUT IS PULLED UP BY THE POWER OF THE CLUB SWINGING PAST THE BODY.

A GOOD FINISH AND A GOOD swing go hand in hand, which is why I suggest that you make a few practice swings before each drive with a focus not on mechanics but on moving your body into a comfortable finish. Make a practice swing, and then pose for the camera and consider how nice the picture will look when you start the real thing. This sounds elementary, but thinking finish first can—and will—have a positive effect on your technique.

THE FINISH

Basically, there are only two positions in the golf swing: the address and the finish. Everything else is a motion and, as such, difficult to analyze. But the finish is static and allows for serious self-analysis. What you want to look for most is balance, which can be achieved only if you've successfully transferred your weight to your front leg, with your right toe gently resting on the turf. In fact, if you're fully balanced, you should be able to tap your right toe on the ground. If you're serious about improving, I suggest performing your driver swing at 50 percent speed until you can end your swing correctly. Then, make a point of holding your finish for 10 seconds. You'll ingrain the sense of what a good finish feels like, while also improving your balance, tempo, and rhythm.

1. A GOOD, BALANCED FINISH SHOULD HAVE THE RIGHT SHOULDER POSITIONED SO THAT IT'S EVEN WITH OR SLIGHTLY AHEAD OF THE LEFT FOOT.

2. A STRAIGHT BACK NOT ONLY PROMOTES GOOD BALANCE, IT'S MUCH EASIER ON YOUR BODY THAN A "REVERSE C" OR A "LUNGING" FINISH.

3. THE RIGHT FOOT SHOULD BE PULLED UP INTO THIS POSITION BY THE ROTATION OF THE BODY IN THE RELEASE.

4. THE KNEES SHOULD BE EVEN WITH ONE ANOTHER, INDICATING THAT YOU'VE FULLY TURNED THROUGH THE SHOT, WITH YOUR BELT BUCKLE FACING THE TARGET.

LESSON 1: BIG, BIGGER, BIGGEST

Over the past 50 years, I've had the privilege to work with some of the greatest players in the game. And I've seen plenty of big hitters in my day. But nothing I had seen could have prepared me for the power demonstrated by long-drive competitor Patrick Dempsey. He approached me in January 2001, looking to add those few extra, precious yards to his already-mammoth drives. After watching Dempsey swing—if you can call propelling the clubhead 140 mph a "swing"—I wasn't quite sure what I could do, until I moved my focus from his technique to his setup. Despite his remarkable athletic ability (Dempsey used to be a professional baseball player) and experience as a professional long driver, his setup was marred by several errors, many of which are common to the setups of even high-handicappers. These flaws were keeping him from his true distance potential. After we hammered them out, Dempsey went on to capture the 2002 RE/MAX World Long Drive Championship in the senior division, with a winning blast of close to 400 yards.

Power comes from a solid foundation (your stance) and the use of that foundation to hit from your right side and through the golf ball. Most golfers limit their ability to hit the ball as far as they can by setting the majority of their weight on the left side at address. If you set up with the majority of your weight forward, it's likely that your left hip will shift away from the target during the backswing instead of turning as it's supposed to, which is a huge power leak. To combat this problem, make sure to set your right shoulder lower than the left. This is an easy way to transfer your weight to your right side on the backswing and to establish a swing path that ultimately ascends into the golf ball—a must to hit the ball high and hard. Setting the right shoulder lower than the left also positions the right elbow inside the left elbow, a prime position that accommodates an aggressive shoulder turn.

A power-rich setup includes a wide base, the head positioned behind the ball, a spine tilt that positions the left shoulder higher than the right, and a right elbow that sits inside the left. These positions not only encourage an aggressive shoulder turn and proper weight shift but facilitate moving the club on an ascending path through the hitting area.

This golfer's big shoulder turn may give the impression of a powerful top position, but he's failed to get his weight fully back on his right side.

If you can't hit the ball from your right side (which is much different from hitting *with* your right side), you'll fall prey to the most damaging power leak of all: coming over the top. An over-the-top swing moves the clubhead from the top position across the golf ball to the left of the target. This sweep-across move not only destroys solid contact but encourages a slice and other ball flight maladies. Plus, if you swing over the top, you're moving your head forward of the ball at impact, which, as we discussed, is a big no-no where the golf swing is concerned.

The root of these errors can be traced to the setup, but even if you can set up properly, you still need the right technique. As you move the club to the top, feel your weight loading over your right foot, with your left shoulder packed tightly underneath your chin. This power-packed state of affairs allows you to store a tremendous amount of power. While most golfers are aware that the shoulders and hips must turn on the backswing, they execute what I like to call a "fake turn." Compare the photos at the left and right. In the left photo, it looks as though the shoulders have rotated, but rotated to where? They have turned in place, stranding weight on the front foot. Now look at the photo at the right. Now that's a turn. Not only have the shoulders correctly rotated, with the left shoulder moving under the chin, but the golfer's weight is firmly planted over the rear foot. All that's left to do is remain on the right side for as long as possible while swinging the club back toward the golf ball, which not only provides more time to square the face but also more time to generate extra clubhead speed.

If asked to, this golfer could lift his left foot off the ground. He's fully loaded, kept a steady head, and turned his left shoulder under his chin.

After you get on your right side at the top of the swing, stay there until the momentum of the club pulls you into the finish.

I spend a lot of hours teaching my students the benefits of a proper setup, the need to make a full-shoulder turn on the backswing, and the importance of getting that weight on the right side. I also tend to go on and on about delaying the rotation of the hips on the downswing and swinging from a packed right side. This may sound complicated, but it's not. All you have to do is keep that head of yours (and thus your upper body) from moving targetward on the downswing. If your head stays behind the ball, you'll be hitting from your right, and that's where you can gain extra clubhead speed and distance and the big drives you've been hoping for.

You'll know you're doing a good job of hanging back when, at impact, you can still see your right foot, while your right shoulder lies just underneath your chin and your hands and clubhead are swinging out toward the target. You literally should be pulled into your finish. To feel the sensation, practice your swing with a golf ball placed under your lead foot. This drill will keep your body from rotating too quickly.

The easiest adjustment a golfer can make to swing faster and hit longer shots is to anchor the head. A normal head weighs 14 pounds. When you put it into motion, it actually creates a lot of force and can pull your entire body along for the ride. And when you move it forward on the downswing, you'll ruin any chance of drawing power from your right side. Steady that head and watch your shots fly high, deep, and straight.

There's an old saying in golf that your address and impact positions should match. While there are certainly some differences between these two positions, I think the statement packs a lot of truth, which is why I teach the setup that I do. Check out the impact photos below. Regardless of your age and/or ability, you can achieve a powerful position at the point of contact, with the hips rotating toward the target, the shoulders lagging behind the hips, and the lead arm in line with the clubshaft and—pay attention here—the head and body back. By keeping the head steady, you'll allow yourself to swing under the body and strike the ball with a big, slightly ascending blow.

It doesn't matter if you're 80 or 18, you can achieve a powerful impact position if you set up properly, hang back, and hit from your right side.

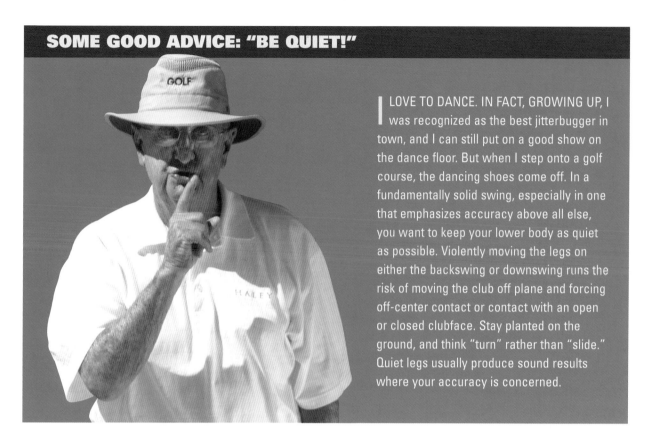

I LOVE TO DANCE. IN FACT, GROWING UP, I was recognized as the best jitterbugger in town, and I can still put on a good show on the dance floor. But when I step onto a golf course, the dancing shoes come off. In a fundamentally solid swing, especially in one that emphasizes accuracy above all else, you want to keep your lower body as quiet as possible. Violently moving the legs on either the backswing or downswing runs the risk of moving the club off plane and forcing off-center contact or contact with an open or closed clubface. Stay planted on the ground, and think "turn" rather than "slide." Quiet legs usually produce sound results where your accuracy is concerned.

LESSON 2: FIND MORE FAIRWAYS

Just 'round the corner from my house in northeastern Oklahoma lies Miami Golf and Country Club, a course on which I grew up and learned the game. It's a track steeped in history, having, at one time, Ky Laffoon as its head professional. I taught each one of my five children to play golf on Miami CC—a course where each hole seems to demand a different golfing skill.

Of course, being in the fairway helps throughout, and like most golf courses, Miami features a hole that forces you to think accuracy first, distance second. The par-4 11th features water to the right, and the area to the left is out of bounds (OB), making it absolutely necessary to produce an accurate drive. I've won my fair share of skins and Nassau bets on number 11 by simply finding the fairway. Whenever the competition swung for the fences, I knew the hole, match or skin, was mine.

I'm sure you know of a hole like number 11 on your home course—a hole where if you're off the fairway, you're in serious trouble. Indeed, there are times when accuracy off the tee is priority number one. When you approach these situations, use the following advice to ensure that you're safe and long.

The accurate driver swing is all about balance, control, and togetherness. In no part of the swing should any part of your body dominate, whether it's the hips, legs, shoulders, or arms. Balance starts at address, where your stance should be slightly wider than shoulder-width and with your feet flared to facilitate your turn. Your right shoulder should hang slightly lower than the left. When the right shoulder sits lower, it makes it much easier to swing from in to out (top left photo on next page).

Also, fight the urge to play the ball too far forward or too far back in your stance. Typically, if you play the ball too far forward, you'll encourage a pull; playing it too far back will encourage a push. Favor a neutral ball position.

As far as the swing goes, there are only a few musts on which to focus. As you move your hands to the top and back through the ball, your upper and lower body should turn but lag behind the hands (top right). A critical point is your approach to the ball. At this point, I like to think of my right arm brushing against my right pocket. This lets me know I'm approaching the ball

from the inside. As I make contact, I should feel my right shoulder hit my chin (photo at right). Here, many golfers raise their heads. This destroys the inside path you worked so hard to create. Instead, let your head rotate toward the target with that right shoulder.

Now that you know what to do, it's a good idea to discuss what not to do. If you can keep from making the following mistakes, you'll have a better chance of hitting your target.

For starters, don't try to over-control your swing by making it too compact. With your short irons, this works well. But the driver is too long for such an approach. In other words, don't pin your right arm to your right side as you would for a delicate approach. Let the right arm float out a bit to create the wider swing arc that the longer-length driver demands. All that I ask is that you point the right elbow toward the ground at the top (don't let it fly out). Again, this makes it easier to maintain the desired inside path.

Also, don't toe dance. Remember your balance. If you're not balanced, one body part is dominating the others, a malady that doesn't apply to accurate driving. Toe dancing occurs when you lift your right foot on the

downswing. Some golfers can get away with this, but most amateurs can't, especially when there's trouble off the fairway. Usually, when you lift up on the right toe, you destroy your swingpath. Same goes for the left foot. When I'm driving the ball well, both my feet are firmly planted as I approach impact.

As you swing past contact, don't forget about your finish. I'm a big believer that most poor drives result from hindering the finish or failing to get to it all together. Never stop rotating toward your target. As you swing to the follow-through, keep in mind that your hands should be traveling toward your target and releasing. Don't quit on it—let that right arm extend and pull your right shoulder through. I know you want to peek to see if your teed ball is safe or not, but fight that tendency. Finish your swing first. Believe me, the ball won't do what you want it to do if you give it an early look.

The main mental challenge is not to assume you're going to pull off a perfect shot. If you've been fading the ball all day, don't expect to suddenly stripe a frozen rope down the center or hit a soft draw. Play the shot the day gave you.

I'm sure you've heard tips on how to generate extra power with the driver, advice such as "drive hard with your lower body" or "whip your shoulders through impact." While these suggestions may give you extra yardage, they simply don't apply if you need to be laser accurate. The accurate driver swing is all about balance, control, and togetherness.

Above all else, if you need an accurate drive, think "accurate from the start." Don't allow tension to creep into your address position. If it does, back off. Take a few continuous practice swings. I like to find some long grass and let my clubhead brush over it, back and through, back and through. Try the same, and see how easily it relaxes your body.

Also, play smart. Guard against your worst shot by teeing up on the side of trouble. If there's OB on the left, tee up on the left side of the box and aim right. Do the opposite if there's trouble on the right. Doing so effectively widens the fairway and creates a greater margin for error.

Last, don't worry about your distance. Remember, you're favoring accuracy here. Keep that your priority. Favor balance over speed, and let your equipment do the work. At about 46 inches, the driver is designed to give you plenty of yards without your consciously giving it that extra juice.

With all this in mind, remember that the driver swing is the most rotational of all. If you get too steep in the forward swing or downswing by limiting the turn of your shoulders and hips, you'll find it difficult to land the ball where you desire. I like to focus on my right leg. Before the start of every swing, I picture it as the center around which my entire body will turn. Combine this thought with active hands and an emphasis on maintaining balance, and you'll be guaranteed the type of shot you need on tight driving holes.

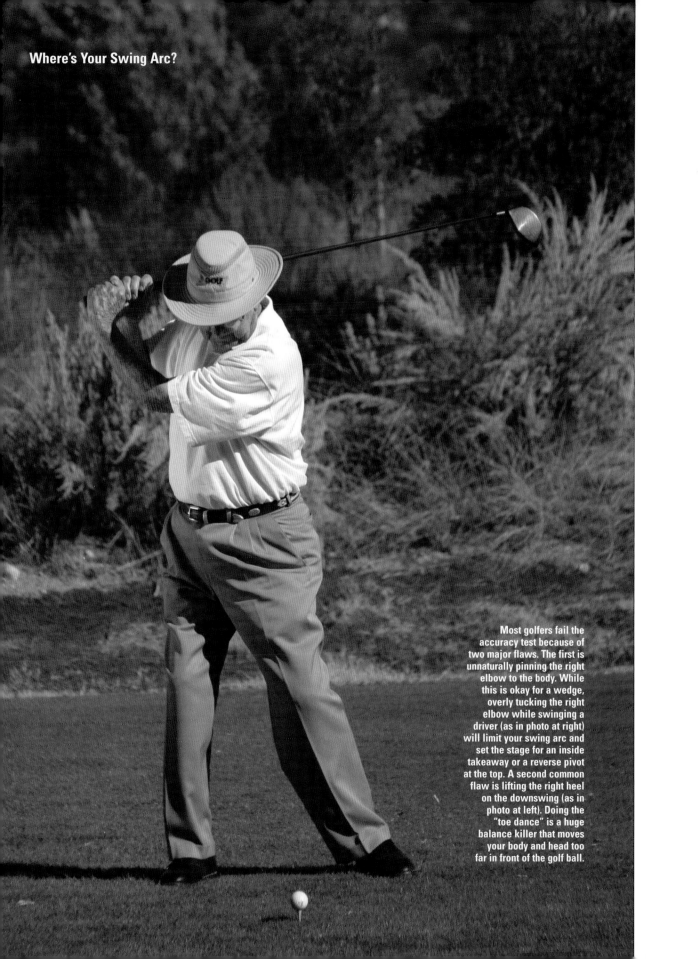

Most golfers fail the accuracy test because of two major flaws. The first is unnaturally pinning the right elbow to the body. While this is okay for a wedge, overly tucking the right elbow while swinging a driver (as in photo at right) will limit your swing arc and set the stage for an inside takeaway or a reverse pivot at the top. A second common flaw is lifting the right heel on the downswing (as in photo at left). Doing the "toe dance" is a huge balance killer that moves your body and head too far in front of the golf ball.

The unfortunate end to an accurate swing starts with sliding the lower body forward on the downswing.

MAKE FAIRWAY WOODS YOUR FRIENDS

5

IN GOLF, PLAYERS ARE TYPICALLY CRITIQUED BY EITHER THEIR DRIVING, IRON PLAY, SHORT GAME, OR PUTTING.

I'm sure you have friends who have a chipping touch but can't get off the tee box, and others who can bomb 'em 280 yards and longer but can't make a putt outside three feet. Every golfer can be labeled as a good, average, or poor driver, ball striker, chipper, putter—whatever. Rarely, however, are golfers defined by their fairway wood play, which is unfortunate because, if used correctly, fairway woods are golf's secret scoring clubs. Their design allows golfers to hit the ball higher and farther than they can with irons, and much more

consistently than with drivers. At 80 years old, I'm still able to shoot my age, thanks to fairway woods. And any respectable tour player knows that a good 3 wood makes tight-driving holes a breeze and can bring any par-5 into range for better scoring opportunities.

I've been teaching golf for more than 50 years, and I've happened to make a few observations. One is that the fairway-wood swing is rarely taught—heck, if you can swing a driver, what's so different about swinging a 3 wood or a 5 wood, right? Wrong. Although fairway

SOME GOOD ADVICE: "SET UP FOR DOWN AND THROUGH!"

WITH FAIRWAY WOODS, YOUR KEY THOUGHT SHOULD BE to hit down and through the ball. Play the ball back—somewhere between the middle of your chest and left shoulder. You'll need to experiment as to exactly where the ball should be played because every golfer's swing arc is different. Make practice swings to determine where your fairway wood bottoms out the most. That's where the ball should be played.

Establishing a perfect fairway wood setup is the best guarantee for a perfect fairway wood swing. The key word is *relax*: relax your right elbow, even going so far as pinning it to your right side. When you do, you'll set your right shoulder lower than your left and establish a swingpath that's inside out (photo at left). Many amateurs make the mistake of tensing up their right arms. The design of the club will give you the distance you need, so don't set up to swing for the fences. Tensing up the right side invariably destroys your setup, most commonly by forcing your left shoulder to open and moving your left elbow inside the right. It all adds up to an outside-in swing and a potential slice (photo at right).

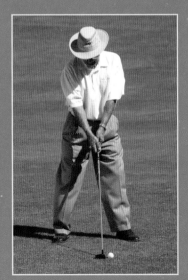
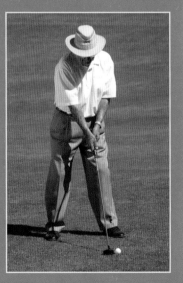

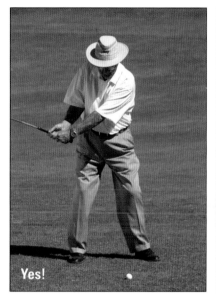

While I advocate hitting down and through with your fairway woods, they shouldn't be swung as upright as you'd do with a wedge or short iron. A fairway wood is the second-longest club in your bag, and the takeaway should accommodate this length. A low, long, one-piece take-away is favored over one where the hands hinge the club at the ball. When you take away the club, think "sweep." On the downswing, think "down and through."

woods are shaped similarly to drivers, their application is much different. In fact, if you had to make a comparison, you should swing your fairway woods more like you do your irons. How many times have you followed up a big drive on a par-5 with a poor 3 wood? The fairway-wood technique is unique, but once you learn it, I guarantee you'll add at least a half dozen options to your shot-making arsenal every round. Interested? Let's get started.

Many of the mistakes I see amateurs make occur in the setup, and the majority of these setup mistakes are the result of one of the biggest myths in golf: you have to hit the ball hard. It's easy to fall into this trap. After all, your 3 wood and 5 wood are much longer than your irons, and certainly the heads are bigger. Consequently, amateurs feel the need to swing hard to get all that length and clubhead size into position at impact. This couldn't be further from the truth. Look at Ernie Els. He swings his woods as easily as he swings his sand wedge. It's only a matter of length—of the club and the swing. Tempo is always the same.

When you set up with the idea that you have to hit the ball hard, it's likely that you'll firm up your right arm at address. I see it happen all the time. The problem with firming the right arm is that it invariably raises the right

shoulder and, as a result, lowers the left. From this type of stance, your hips and shoulders will automatically align themselves to the left of your target and force a swing that's outside in. You know the typical result here to be a slice.

The fairway wood swing, like all swings, needs to be inside out. In order to hit inside out, you need to be set up to do so, and when you drop the left shoulder, you're as far away from being able to hit to the outside as possible. Instead, forget about firming the right side and trying to hit the ball hard. The length of the club will take care of distance, so concentrate on your swing and the inside-out path you need to create.

The best example of a perfect fairway-wood setup is the one utilized by Corey Pavin. At address, he keeps his right elbow nice and relaxed, and nearly pinned to his side. Not only does this negate tension, but it positions his left shoulder higher than his right.

As far as ball position is concerned, don't fall into the bad habit of playing the ball too far forward. Most recreational golfers play the ball when setting up to swing their fairway woods as they'd do with their drivers. I know the clubs are similarly shaped, but the driver is longer and needs to be played forward. Plus, the driver swing motion is an upward-sweeping motion, and you need that extra little bit of distance to power your driver up and through the ball.

As I mentioned in the previous chapter, the driver swing arc is a sweeping, ascending arc. On the other hand, the fairway wood swing arc needs to be more like the ones you create with your irons: descending. A good rule of thumb to apply is that anytime the ball is on the ground, you need to go down and through it, not sweep it. Even when you tee up a fairway wood, tee it low and swing down and through. Now, you don't have to take a huge divot with your 3 wood as you should when you hit down and through with your irons and wedges, but don't be afraid to do so.

As far as swing technique is concerned, the key word is *synchronization*. Synchronization may not be the simplest word in the dictionary, but it makes for a simple, effective swing. If I were to learn the game all over again and have someone tell me to shift my weight, turn my hips, raise my hands, drop my arms, clear my hips, fire my right side, and shift my weight laterally, I probably would take up a different sport. If you're reading this book, I'm sure you have a good idea how to swing the club properly. If you're still having trouble, it's probably because you're not synchronizing your swing. And it's probably why your fairway-wood game suffers—the longer the club, the more a lack of synchronization will hurt you.

1. KEEP YOUR RIGHT SHOULDER LOWER THAN YOUR LEFT AT ADDRESS AND THROUGH THE DOWNSWING. WHEN YOU DO, YOU'LL CREATE THE DESIRED INSIDE-TO-OUT SWINGPATH AND TONS OF FAIRWAY-WOOD POWER.

2. A NICE, RELAXED RIGHT ELBOW IS KEY FOR AN EFFECTIVE FAIRWAY-WOOD SWING. IF IT'S STRAIGHT AT ADDRESS, YOU'LL DESTROY YOUR ALIGNMENT AND SET IN MOTION A SLICE-CAUSING PATH. KEEP IT BENT UNTIL AFTER IMPACT.

3. IN A GOOD FAIRWAY-WOOD SWING, THE HANDS LEAD. IN FACT, IN ALL GOOD GOLF SWINGS, THE HANDS LEAD. JUST REMEMBER TO SYNCHRONIZE THEIR MOVEMENT WITH THE ROTATION OF YOUR SHOULDERS AND HIPS.

4. MAINTAIN A SOLID LOWER BODY. ON THE BACKSWING, FIGHT THE URGE TO OVER-TURN YOUR HIPS—KEEP THAT FORWARD KNEE STEADY. ON THE WAY BACK TO THE BALL, KEEP THE REAR FOOT FLAT UNTIL YOUR SWING PULLS IT UP.

5. FIGHT THE HABIT OF PLAYING THE BALL TOO FAR FORWARD—OFF THE LOGO OF YOUR SHIRT IS PERFECT. IF YOU PLAY THE BALL TOO MUCH TOWARD YOUR TOE, YOU'LL RISK PULLING OR CATCHING THE BALL THINLY.

When practicing your fairway-wood technique, remember to lead with your hands. This is great news because your hands are the easiest part of your body to control. You've been using your hands since the day you were born. Use that to your advantage. On the backswing, swing your hands back and, at the same time, allow your left shoulder to turn in front of you. If you concentrate on these two moves, you'll find that, without any extra movement, your weight will be firmly established on your right side at the top of the backswing, just where it needs to be.

On the way down, again lead with your hands. I don't recommend that you power your lower-body turn or clear your hips—leave that to the pros. Rather, swing with your hands, and, as they reach hip level on the downswing, turn your hips right along with them.

I ask my students to "wear their right pockets out." That is, on the downswing, sense that the hands are brushing against the front of the right hip. As your hands brush against your pocket, start turning your hips in sync with the downward motion of your hands. Not only does this keep the clubhead from moving off plane, but it guards against too much lateral sliding (the number one cause of a slice) and better allows you to hit down and through the ball. Through the impact area, your hands and hips should be in unison, and your right shoulder, if you brushed your hands against the right pocket, should brush the underside of your chin. Simple.

As you make contact with the ball, don't try to get fancy. Don't force your release or overemphasize the need to rotate your forearms or whatever you've been told to do. If you synchronize your hands and hips and turn your left shoulder back and your right shoulder through, you'll strike the ball fine, and your release will take care of itself. When you swing, what happens after impact occurs naturally—good players never think about their follow-through. They focus on what comes before it and allow it to simply happen. Only when you try to "hit" the ball will you have to make compensations that, more often than not, spell disaster.

LESSON 1: CHECK YOUR GEAR

As we inch deep into this new millennium, society's fascination with technology certainly affects the way our game is played. While the use of titanium for driver

heads led the technology charge in the late 1990s, the game's acceptance of hybrid woods and higher-lofted fairway woods—and the designs employed to help these types of clubs outperform their long-iron counterparts—has been the big story of the past few years.

High-lofted fairway woods have been popular additions to players' bags, and I'm sure you own a few yourself (1 carry five woods, including a driver). These clubs are easier to hit, and they launch the ball higher than the long irons they replace. So what's the big deal about hybrids, also designed to replace the more-difficult-to-hit long irons? Isn't a high-lofted fairway wood just as good as one of the new hybrid models? The answer is yes and no. Your typical fairway wood is much longer than your typical hybrid, and longer always means less control. In most cases, the new hybrids feature shorter, iron-type shafts for better control. And because the shafts are shorter, the heads can be made heavier. This luxury enables designers to move more mass to the low and rear areas of the clubhead, increasing launch angle and reducing both side- and backspin. Plus, the compact hybrid head shape is well suited for a variety of lies. In the end, a hybrid is a more useful club for the recreational player.

If you find yourself among the many who want to take advantage of the hybrids' versatility but are somewhat confused as to how to use them, don't worry, you're not the only one. The big question technique-wise I hear the most is, "If you're supposed to hit down on the ball with your irons and slightly up on the ball with your fairway woods, what in the world do you do with a hybrid club?"

The key to swinging a hybrid club correctly is to look at which club(s) the hybrid has replaced. Because most hybrids are designed to replace irons, I advise golfers to swing them just as they would irons. Furthermore, most of the specs for weight, loft, lie, length, and the shaft match iron specs.

Practice making a few swings with your hybrid as if it were an iron, and remember that it's not necessary to scoop the ball upward (as many feel they have to do with low-lofted, long irons). Instead, allow the low and deep center of gravity to work its magic and launch the ball at a high and optimal angle. The trick? Don't be afraid to swing down and through as you would with an iron.

If you use a hybrid off the tee in the middle of a round, take at least four practice swings to adjust to the different weight and feel of the club—particularly when you've been hitting woods for consecutive holes. Tee up the ball higher than you would a normal iron to make it easier to achieve square contact. Finally, swing with a moderate tempo.

LESSON 2: DON'T FORGET ABOUT LONG IRONS

If you're like most golfers, your long irons are the most feared—and most misunderstood—clubs in your bag. They don't have to be. The long iron is a valuable weapon to own, and I don't care who you are, there's nothing more satisfying than hitting a long-iron shot right on the nose. It's the best-looking shot in golf, with its nice, flat trajectory and a feeling in your hands that

you just can't describe. The problem comes when you don't trust your club to do the work.

When my students pick up a 3 or 4 iron, I can frequently see the tension in their faces. Then they try to help get the ball airborne rather than letting the loft of the club take care of it. This results in all kinds of bad shots—and more fear. Your long irons can help you score on the golf course, but only if you overcome your nerves and learn to treat them like friends instead of enemies.

Though I'm getting up there in years, I can remember when almost everyone carried a 2 iron, and a lot of folks even packed 1 irons in their bags. Thanks to modern equipment technology, that's simply not the case anymore. These days, with the proliferation of 5, 7, 9, and even 11 woods in the bags of players of all abilities, as well as the rise in popularity of hybrid woods and irons, even the 3 iron is sometimes relegated to the garage or the trunk of the car.

Regardless, I'm a firm believer that long irons still have a place in golf. You just have to be smart about the design you choose. Make sure that your long irons are cavity-backed and perimeter-weighted. Blade models may be okay for short irons and wedges, but there's no sense in trying to hit a long-iron shot with a blade club. Unless you're a pro, you'll be thankful for the extra forgiveness you'll get with a cavity back.

For most of my students, I wouldn't recommend carrying anything longer than a 3 iron; usually, I'd suggest a 5 or 7 wood. However, a less-lofted iron does have certain advantages over higher-lofted woods. A good long-iron player has much greater trajectory control and shot-shaping ability with a long iron than with a 7 wood. If you live in an area where the wind blows, your long irons will allow you to hit shots (boring, wind-cheating shots, for example) that high-lofted woods can't pull off. Also, long irons are great off the tee on short doglegs and other layup holes where you need to bend the ball. The bottom line is, you have to be able to hit the long irons you do carry, even if they're only a 4 and 5 iron.

You can easily improve your long-iron play just by making three simple changes to your address position.

First, play the ball farther up in your stance, opposite your left heel. Unlike shorter clubs, where you want to

Yes: Ball Forward

Yes: Open Face

Yes: Open Stance

No: Ball Back

No: Squared Face

No: Squared Stance

hit down into the ball to impart spin, you want to sweep the ball off the ground with a long iron while taking only a small amount of turf, very similar to what you need with a fairway-wood shot. Playing the ball off the left heel sets up the sweeping motion and helps delay your release through the hitting area.

Second, open your stance ever so slightly by drawing your left foot back a bit from the target line. By doing this, you'll add a little delay to your release. It doesn't seem like much, but it means the clubface has an even greater chance of being square when it reaches the golf ball so that you can use the entire loft of the club.

Finally, turn the clubface a couple of degrees open. I even have my pro-level students do this. Don't worry that you're going to slice the ball. You won't. Instead, you'll ease your mind because you'll be able to see some evidence of loft on the clubface, and you won't feel as though you have to work to get the ball into the air. You'll also be promoting a good release. Trust me, the clubface will naturally return to a square position as you swing through and release.

After you've made you setup adjustments, all you have to do is treat the long iron as you would any other club in your bag. Now I know that's easy to say, so here are a few keys to focus on when you're practicing with your long irons.

Use your left knee to set your tempo on the backswing. As you take away the club, make sure that your clubhead, left knee, hands, and shoulders all move together. When they do, it means that you won't have to play catch-up with either your body or the club later in the swing.

Let your shoulders turn the body. Most golfers tend to over-turn—especially with their lower bodies. Over-turning flattens out your swing plane and keeps you from getting set powerfully behind the golf ball. Instead, concentrate on turning your left shoulder so that it points to the ground behind the ball at the top of the swing. Your lower body will do all of the turning it needs to on its own.

Pause for a moment at the top of the swing. Now everything—your hands, body, and club—can work together on the downswing. As you start back toward the golf ball, let your hands drop so that your right

elbow feels as though it's sweeping through the right pocket of your pants.

Be sure to stand tall. Too many golfers lunge with their bodies from the top of the swing and end up in an impact position that makes solid contact impossible. You want to stand tall and stay behind the ball. The release will come naturally. Your momentum will carry you all the way through impact (photo above), with your right shoulder passing underneath your chin. Stay down and through the ball, and let the clubhead carry you into a nice, balanced finish.

PUTT FOR SHOW, DOUGH—WHATEVER

6

PUTTING IS THE BLACK MAGIC OF GOLF. BEN HOGAN SAID IT SHOULD BE A SEPARATE GAME.

Sam Snead probably would have agreed. On the other hand, Bobby Jones believed that putting should make the difference. All I know is this: the folks who are winning tournaments are the folks who are making putts.

Aside from helping to win tournaments, improved putting is a surefire way to cut shots off your score. Unfortunately, most players spend their practice time beating balls on the range, ignoring the one club that can make the difference between winning and losing. Think back to your best-scoring rounds or the times you really cleaned up in your regular weekend game. I can almost guarantee that the flatstick was the key to your success.

Putting is the most individual element in golf. All you have to do is watch the pros on television to see that there's not necessarily a right or wrong way to do it. Bobby Locke was one of the greatest putters of all time, although his wristy technique broke many of the "rules"

to which more conventional putters generally adhere. I wouldn't recommend his stroke to anyone, but it worked for him. And that's the bottom line—if you're making a lot of putts, don't change a thing. You're probably doing it right. If not, however, listen up.

All the great golfers I've known owned a closet full of putters. Putting is all about confidence, and sometimes you just need to look down and see something new in order to believe you're going to putt well. Besides, I want my putter to know that it's supposed to work well for me. If it doesn't, I won't wait a second before I throw it into the closet with all the others.

Regardless of which putter you use, you should know how to find its sweet spot. When you strike the ball on the sweet spot, you get a true roll. Hitting the ball on the heel or toe of the putter will cause the face to twist ever so slightly and will decrease your chances of making the putt. Find the sweet spot by holding the putter with the face pointing up. Bounce a

SOME GOOD ADVICE: "SHORTEN THAT STROKE"

A KEY TO SOLID PUTTING IS ACCELERATION, which means the putterhead should be gaining speed as it approaches the golf ball. A lot of golfers are guilty of decelerating, which can cause tons of on-green misery. Decelerating usually results from making too long of a backstroke. I suggest that you shorten your stroke and focus on accelerating from there. With a shorter backstroke length, you'll become more aware of "powering" the putterhead into impact. Place a tee in the ground just outside the right foot, making sure with each practice stroke you swing the putter no further than the tee.

ball on the face until you determine where the sweet spot is—you'll feel it in your hands and fingers. Then, take a magic marker and make a small mark on the topline of your putter, directly above the sweet spot, and make sure that's where you line up every time. Don't assume the sweet spot of your putter resides in the center of the putterface.

If you don't already have a regular pre-putt routine, you should work to develop one. My routine starts as soon as I mark my ball after reaching the green. I clean the ball to make sure it will roll properly, and then I crouch down behind the mark to study the line of the putt. I work all the weather conditions and land characteristics into my read. Finally, I pick the line and visualize the ball rolling along it until it drops in the hole. When I replace my ball, I line up the ball's seam with the line of the putt. After two practice strokes, I'm ready to pull the trigger with confidence.

Open Putterface

Of course, all the expert green reading in the world won't save you if you can't line up the putter to your target line. The mistake I see people make—amateurs and professionals alike—is not using the entire putterface for alignment. Make sure that both the heel and toe are at right angles to the line of the putt to ensure you're aimed properly.

After you've learned how to line up square to your target line, you can experiment with the clubface just as you do when you need to hit a fade or a draw with a longer club. For sharp right-to-left putts, I might open the clubface slightly to make sure the ball starts high and works its way back down to the hole. For sharp left-to-right putts, I might close the putterface a little, again to make sure that the ball starts above the hole or on what's commonly referred to as the "pro side." Watch the good putters you know: it will amaze you how many putts they make in the sides of the hole. That's because they play on the "pro side."

Square Putterface

Closed Putterface

Here's some simple putting physics: your putts will travel in the direction the putterface points. With that in mind, it's critical to align the putterface perpendicularly to your target line at address. Look to the center, heel, and toe of the putterhead to properly align the putterface, and favor models with easily recognizable sight lines to help accomplish this simple—yet crucial—task. It's amazing how many golfers align the face either open or closed to the target. And these same golfers wonder why they miss so many putts.

If you're at all familiar with my teaching philosophy, you know that I stress one thing on all shots—acceleration. That's true with putting as well. The right shoulder has to stay in motion as you accelerate through the ball. By keeping the shoulder moving—think of it as your putterface—you'll lessen the chance of quitting on the stroke. Remember, when it comes to putting, deceleration is your worst enemy.

You can use whichever grip feels good—reverse overlap, split-handed, cross-handed, etc. Some of the best putters I know use the "old man's" grip, with the index finger on the lower hand pointing straight down the shaft. I like to turn my hands slightly underneath the putter grip because it helps me keep them from breaking down at impact.

There are as many styles of putting as there are golfers, but I've been around long enough to see what all the good putters have in common. First, all good putters keep their eyes focused straight down on the back of the ball. If you let your eyes follow the clubhead back and through the stroke, you'll have problems. Another thing I've noticed is that most of the best putters I've seen stand fairly tall, with just a little knee bend at address. This helps you see the line more clearly. Keep your eyes focused, your head steady, and your posture fixed throughout the entire stroke, and then just concentrate on hitting the ball with authority. That's how Ray Floyd, Bobby Locke, Bob Charles, and all of golf's great putters do it.

I'm sure you've heard people say that you should always swing the same way on the golf course. On the putting green, however, that's not quite true. Depending on the length of the putt, I alter both my grip and my stroke. For short putts, I prefer a slightly firmer grip and a "pop" stroke that will rap the ball into the back of the cup. For longer putts, grip the putter a little more loosely and take a slightly longer stroke. Try to pour longer putts over the edge of the hole.

In my opinion, any golfer can learn to make a decent putting stroke with just a little amount of work. What takes time to develop—sometimes years—is distance control. You know you have control problems if on one day you can never get to the cup and the next you're blowing it by three and four feet. Learning how far back to take the putterhead to hit a putt a specific

When it comes to putting, deceleration is your worst enemy. To lessen the chance of quitting on the putt, keep your right shoulder in motion all the way through impact.

distance (made even more difficult by varying slopes and grass types) takes time, but even those who learn this art may still suffer control problems because they add or subtract loft from what's built into the putterface (loft of four degrees has proved optimal at impact). Every putter is built with a certain degree of loft. If you come into the ball on an ascending arc, you'll add loft to the putter, causing the ball to rise more than usual and reduce the distance that it would travel had you hit it squarely. If you come into the ball with a descending arc, you'll subtract loft from the putterface. The typical result of this scenario is that the ball travels farther than normal.

A compound problem arises if you're adding loft to the club, realize all of your putts are coming up short, and you add some force to your stroke. Here's where distance control can really turn your hair gray. You'll never adequately know how far your putts travel unless you can learn to consistently strike the ball squarely with the amount of loft that's built into your putterface. That's why I advocate a simple stroke. Some golfers like to raise the putterhead in the backstroke and drop it in the forward stroke. In my opinion, this makes it all too easy to change the loft of the face as contact with the ball is made. The key is to keep the putterhead low to the ground throughout the entire stroke. If the height of your putter varies throughout your putting motion, you're only asking for trouble. Unless you have robot-like reflexes, you'll hit most of your putts with different degrees of putterface loft, making the task of controlling the distance of your putts nearly impossible.

The one-hand drill: set up about five feet away from the hole and, using just your right hand, putt until you sink five balls in a row. This drill will help you develop feel and a smooth, pendulum stroke. Keep that putterhead low to the ground throughout.

LESSON 1: PUTTING PRACTICE

The putting stroke is all about tempo. Your body and head should remain perfectly still, with your hands and shoulders doing all of the work. Some people possess an inherent sense of perfect tempo. Others don't and need to spend time on the practice putting green to develop a better sense of rhythm and touch. These drills will certainly help.

The one-hand drill: set up about five feet away from the hole and, using just your right hand, practice until you can sink five balls in a row. This drill will help you get a feel for a smooth, pendulum stroke.

The speed drill: stand at the center of the putting green with four balls. Now putt to the edge of the green. It's like pitching pennies—you want to come as close to the fringe as you can without touching it. Remember, speed is always more important than line on long putts—this drill will help you get a feel for speed.

"Pop and recoil" drill: how often do you get careless and take a decelerating wave at a short putt? Once per round is way too much! Practice from two feet away. The idea is to "pop" the ball

and then return the putter to the address position before the ball hits the back of the hole. This will teach you the kind of compact, accelerating stroke you need to make all of your short putts.

If you're already putting well, don't go changing based on these observations. Just keep making putts. I believe you should hole everything out—that's the only way to really gain the confidence you'll need in competition. Also, practice everywhere. In your golfing life, you're going to encounter all kinds

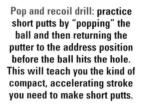

Pop and recoil drill: **practice short putts by "popping" the ball and then returning the putter to the address position before the ball hits the hole. This will teach you the kind of compact, accelerating stroke you need to make short putts.**

of surfaces—fast, slow, grainy, bumpy. You've got to adapt. I tell my students to practice in hotel rooms, on their wood floors at home, on the concrete in the garage. Putting is all about feel, and any surface you have at hand can help you develop it.

LESSON 2: GREEN READING

Once your ball is on the green, you should immediately start taking note of the factors that could influence the putt. For instance, what's the general lay of the land around the green? Can you see a distinct slope or drainage area that will affect the roll of the ball? How much water is on the green? What

Speed drill: **stand at the center of the putting green with four balls. Now putt to the edge of the green, coming as close to the fringe as you can without touching it. This drill will help you develop a feel for speed.**

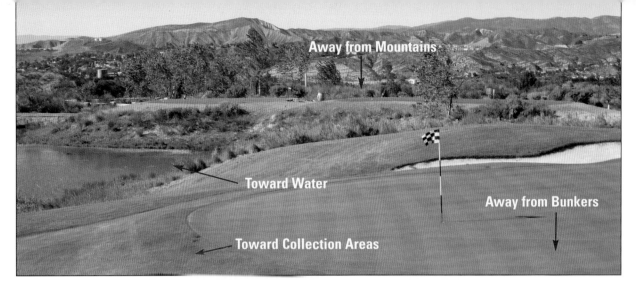

Away from Mountains

Toward Water

Away from Bunkers

Toward Collection Areas

All other effects considered, the environment surrounding the courses on which you play can determine the direction your ball travels after it's struck. Here's a quick outline of how Mother Nature can affect your putts: 1. Putts will tend to break (or move faster) away from surrounding mountains and, in most instances, greenside bunkers. 2. Putts will tend to break (or move faster) toward the nearest water, whether it's a lake, pond, river, or the Pacific Ocean. 3. Putts tend to break (or move faster) toward obvious drainage areas; look for particularly wet sections around the green or for flood channels. 4. Putts will tend to break (or move faster) toward the sun because grass grows toward the sunshine, enhancing the effect of grain.

do seasonal changes do to the speed and the break of the green? Is there a prevailing wind? You'll need to take all of these elements into account as you determine the line of the putt. Sometimes there's a fine line between holing a putt and lipping out, and you never know which bit of information will make the difference.

Take a good look at the whole green as you approach it. Often I find that from a distance, I can get a pretty good idea of the lie of the land, and that's my first clue as to what breaks the ball might take.

Look from behind the ball and look from the side. It needn't take long—if you're smart you can usually find time in between your playing partners hitting their approach shots and their putts.

Look at what your playing partner's ball does as it approaches the hole. Even if he or she isn't coming from exactly the same line as you are, you can still learn a lot about how the ball behaves in that crucial last 18 inches or so of its journey to the hole.

Remember, speed determines break. A firmly struck putt breaks less than a ball hit at a slower speed. So decide how firmly you want to hit the putt, and then establish how much the ball will move at that speed. In the end, you should leave yourself with a tap-in, should you miss the cup.

LESSON 3: FIVE PUTTING MISTAKES . . . AND HOW TO AVOID THEM

Putting is for scoring. You won't need to drive the ball 300 yards on every hole, and you don't need an accurately placed wedge shot into every green, either. What you do need is a solid putting stroke, one that continually gets the ball within tap-in range at the very worst. If we all 3-putted less, our scores would be much lower without having to make a single change to our full swings. Avoid these mistakes on the putting green at all costs.

MISTAKE #1: BAD READS

Green reading is a tough area of the game to teach. It takes practice. It takes experience. But even golfers with long playing careers fail to judge the appropriate break because they look for break in all the wrong places. Most focus solely on the area around the hole.

True, the ground around the cup will influence the roll, but don't forget about other break influences, such as the area where your ball lies or collection areas off the green. Look for drainage areas. If the course sits near a large geographical landmark (an ocean, mountain, etc.), keep in mind that these will greatly affect break. Plan accordingly.

MISTAKE #2: OPEN PUTTERFACE

You can't set up to putt with an open face. If you do, you'll miss to the right every time, regardless of the quality of your stroke.

Use the club's painted sight lines or natural aiming lines to align your putter perpendicularly to the target line, and consider these lines when shopping for a new putter. Find a putter that feels good, of course, but also one that's easy to align. We're all likely to try something that works well for our playing partners or our favorite professional player. Don't fall into that trap. Experiment and find a putter that works for you. It may be something you'd never previously considered owning.

MISTAKE #3: DECELERATION

You have a three-foot putt to win a match on the final hole. It's a straight putt. A no-brainer. But it comes up short or drifts just below the right edge. What happened? If you're like the majority of recreational players, you decelerated, the worst of all putting errors. It's easy to do on short putts, where we've all been guilty of trying to "baby" the ball into the hole.

Your putting stroke, regardless of the length of the putt, always should accelerate at a constant rate. The manner in which you alter distance is by changing the length of your backstroke and throughstroke. Whatever the length, your putterhead should gain speed through the contact zone.

MISTAKE #4: POOR STANCE

1. **SITUATE YOUR BODY SO THAT YOUR EYES ARE DIRECTLY OVER THE BALL AND YOUR HEAD IS IN LINE WITH YOUR SPINE.**

2. **BALANCE YOUR WEIGHT EVENLY OVER YOUR FEET, WITH YOUR ARMS HANGING NATURALLY FROM THEIR SOCKETS.**

3. **HOLD THE PUTTER IN YOUR PALMS AND PLAY THE BALL MIDSTANCE.**

Putting is personal, and you should adopt a stance that is comfortable to you. But I suggest that you follow the stance fundamentals pictured in the photos above. If you do, you'll be in a lot better position to make the kinds of strokes that produce the truest rolls and putts that stay true to the line.

Don't make the mistake of making comfort and ease your primary concern when putting.

MISTAKE #5: RIGHT SHOULDER STOPS

Contrary to public opinion, the putterhead should "release" along the target line, much as your iron or driver head does in the full swing. This release is a natural reaction to the putterhead accelerating through impact and moving the ball along the intended line. One of the reasons golfers fail to accelerate is that they stop the movement of their right shoulder after impact.

To properly accelerate and release the putter-head, the right shoulder must continue to move down the target line following contact. If you stop your right shoulder, your right hand will take over and lift up the putterhead and increase the chance of striking the top half of the golf ball, producing more skid than roll.

LESSON 4: CHECK YOUR GEAR

In order to become the best putter you can be, you must find the right putter. Like all golfers, I've tried all kinds of models, favoring the ones that, above all other considerations, simply felt "good" in my hands. Today's putter market offers thousands of options, some with shapes more suited for tending the garden than rolling a golf ball into the hole. If you want my advice, look for putters with a lot of straight edges and perpendicular lines. These types of flatsticks make it so much easier to align the club square to your target line. I've always used a PING Anser or similarly shaped putter. Their shape makes it simple to point the putterhead in the right direction.

Also, focus on the hosel, the portion of the putter that connects the clubhead to the shaft. Hosel shape and location often have the most significant effect on how the club actually swings. Knowing the difference between one hosel design and another can be of value when choosing a new putter (certain types of configurations tend to work for different types of strokes) and also can provide some insight into your stroke and what type of putter you are. Here's what to look for:

Plumber-neck: Popularized by the original PING Anser, the plumber-neck is characterized by a horizontal bend just below where the end of the shaft and the hosel meet. This design, which generally provides a medium amount of offset, does a great job of keeping the hands ahead of the clubhead through impact. This tends to make the putter more forgiving and easier to use, which is the reason it's so popular. Putters with plumber-neck hosels tend to be somewhat toe-down in

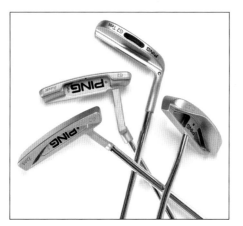

their weighting scheme, which encourages a slightly inside-square-inside stroke.

Flare-tip: The flare-tip is typically a "shaft-over" hosel, meaning the shaft covers the top of the hosel where the two connect. Putters with flare-tip hosels generally have less offset and are more blade-like in their design. These putters tend to be quite a bit toe-down in their weighting scheme and usually work best for golfers who like to rotate the blade open and shut through the stroke. If you like blade putters, such as the venerable Wilson 8802, then a flare-tip hosel might be worth a look.

No hosel: Face-balanced putters often have no hosel but instead have an S-bend shaft that goes directly into the putterhead. These putters are designed specifically for golfers who want to take the club straight back and straight through in a piston-like motion. If you typically like to rotate the clubhead during your stroke, these types of putters probably won't work as well for you, although there are no absolutes in this regard. The popular Odyssey 2-Ball mallet is a good example of a no-hosel putter.

Long hosel: These designs are usually elongated plumber-necks and are used to create face-balancing. Although they look very similar to the standard plumber-neck design, the extra length definitely creates a different feel, which you should take into consideration before selecting a putter with this type of hosel structure. Be aware that the elongated plumber-neck design doesn't always result in face-balancing; many, in fact, are toe-balanced.

Slant-neck: These hosels often are plumber-necks that bend back from the shaft line. Usually, this type of putter is used to create a more substantial amount of offset, which promotes more of an upward strike into the golf ball. Another beneficial aspect of the slant-neck design is the position it places the hands just prior to, and through, impact. Maintaining a hand position that's just slightly in front of the ball is critical to solid putting, and the slant-neck design is an effective way to accomplish this.

SIMPLE SHOT-MAKING

7

THE AVERAGE PGA TOUR PLAYER MISSES THE GREEN ROUGHLY 35 PERCENT OF THE TIME.

This same mythical, average player makes par or better after missing the green about six times out of 10. As a result, this player makes about three bogeys per round, not counting 3-putting a green hit in regulation. Using the median birdie average, your everyday pro can still break par despite missing every third green. Now, I'm willing to bet that (1) you miss more than six greens a round, and (2) you don't get up and down six times out of 10, if and when you do. Of course, the more greens you hit, the more likely it is that you'll post good scores. But, as you've just learned, even the best players in the world miss their fair share of greens. That's why it's important to be able to save par from anywhere on the course.

I remember when Craig Stadler played in the 1994 PGA Championship at Southern Hills Country Club in Tulsa, Oklahoma. The first day he hit only seven greens in regulation but still shot a 70. The next day he hit four greens and shot another 70. The third day he struck the ball beautifully and hit 13 greens. I'll give you one guess what his score was. That's right, another 70.

The lesson is: you can get a lot out of your game even when it's not running on all cylinders. And the only way to do that is think "par" first and "miracle" second. You'll always find yourself in a few bad spots on the course during every round. The key is knowing which shot to play to make the most out of a difficult situation. And it all starts with building a repertoire of "must-have" shots, both with your long clubs and with your wedges. Over the next several pages, we'll take a look at different situations to provide you with all you need to make the right club selection and to use the right technique to match the situation at hand. We'll try to get you that par or, if things work out perfectly, a birdie.

THE FADE

Unless you play golf only in the desert, you're going to encounter some tree trouble and, therefore, must have the ability to bend the ball on command. Plus, it's always a great idea to be able to curve the ball away from trouble (water, bunkers, etc.) when all that's required is a safe shot. Enter the fade and the draw.

People often confuse a fade with a slice, but that's hardly the case. Just ask Jack Nicklaus, who made himself a legend with his left-to-right shot shape. True, you won't get as much distance on the fade, so hit one more club. And, if the wind is blowing more than five mph, your shot is liable to be knocked off-line because the ball is higher,

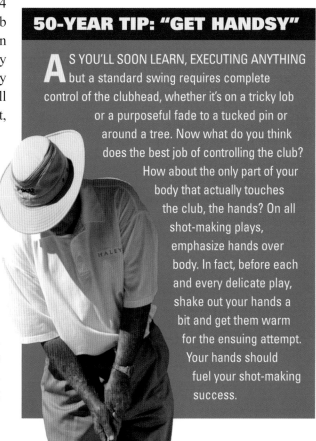

50-YEAR TIP: "GET HANDSY"

AS YOU'LL SOON LEARN, EXECUTING ANYTHING but a standard swing requires complete control of the clubhead, whether it's on a tricky lob or a purposeful fade to a tucked pin or around a tree. Now what do you think does the best job of controlling the club? How about the only part of your body that actually touches the club, the hands? On all shot-making plays, emphasize hands over body. In fact, before each and every delicate play, shake out your hands a bit and get them warm for the ensuing attempt. Your hands should fuel your shot-making success.

The simplest way to execute a fade is to set up by first pointing the clubface at your target and then arranging your feet along a line that points toward the direction you want the ball to start.

To bend the ball from left to right, swing along the direction of your toe line (from slightly outside to in), and finish with the shaft pointing straight up.

exposing it to the wind longer. If the wind is very strong, your fade may not have the velocity to keep it on track because it's hit with an open clubface, which produces a softer shot. For this reason, in heavy winds, it's a good idea to take your chances and play low shots to the centers of the greens, no matter where the pins are.

In my opinion, people make shot-shaping too much of an exact science. Whenever Stadler needed to hit a fade or draw, he simply thought "fade" or "draw." It really is in the mind's eye, but here are a few keys nonetheless.

Setup: Aim your clubface at the target, and align your body so that it's open and angled to the left. Sole your club using only your right hand, take your setup, and then put your left hand on without changing your aim. Grip the club firmly, especially with the left hand. This keeps your clubface from shutting down through impact.

Swing: Swing in the direction your shoulders are aligned, creating an outside-to-in swingpath. Because your clubface points down the target line at address, it's open to the path of your club at impact, so your shot starts left and curves back to the target.

Finish: Finish with your knuckles aimed at the sky and the shaft of your club pointing to the right of target for a major-league fade. Finish with the shaft pointing straight up and down to create a more modest curve.

"The secrets to pulling off a fade all take place in the setup."

The simplest way to execute a draw is to set up by first pointing the clubface at your target and then arranging your feet along a line that points in the direction you want the ball to start.

To bend the ball from right to left, make an aggressive swing along the direction of your toe line and rotate the toe of the club over the heel.

THE DRAW

Every golfer should learn how to hit a draw on command. It's the most powerful shot in golf and almost always features a bit more run than other types of ball flights. Plus, it enforces the slightly inside-out swing necessary on most full-swing shots. Again, the demands of hitting a draw all can be taken care of in the setup.

Setup: Before setup, aim your clubface at the target using only your left hand. When your clubface is in position, keep it there and place your right hand on the club. Align your body parallel to the "line of start." Because you've pulled your right foot back, adjust your stance by moving closer to the ball. If you're set up correctly, your clubface points where you want your ball to finish (the target), and your body points in the direction you want the ball to start (to the right). Lighten your grip pressure.

Swing: One of the keys to shot-making is to take care of your direction at address and then concentrate on producing the correct distance with your swing. Never try to produce direction with your swing. To produce a right-to-left curve, you'll have to deliver an aggressive blow with the toe rotating over the heel of your club. Don't flip your wrists at the ball. Allow the momentum of your clubhead to rotate your forearms.

Finish: The signature of the draw is the finish, with the back of your right hand pointing up and your right arm stretched fully in front of your chest.

"Never baby a draw. Get aggressive and use those hands to rotate the face through impact."

USING THE GREEN

For this shot, let's say you either shorted the green or came up way long. Your lie is good, but you still have 20 or so yards to the pin. Do you fly it all the way to the hole with a wedge? Should you plan for any spin? You can certainly opt to play these types of shots, but if you're looking to get up and down for par, then grab your 8 iron.

Set up as you would to stroke a putt, with your body turned slightly open, with a choked-down grip, and with a little forward press of the hands. More important, hood the face or, in other words, turn it counterclockwise so that it's closed. By closing the face, you'll keep the ball lower to the ground. In my opinion, chipping the ball with an 8 or 9 iron so that it rolls the majority of the way to the cup is the best way to cover long distances around the green.

The swing motion for this shot is similar to a putting stroke. Keep the club on line on both the backswing and forward swing, and move the club with a constant rate of speed. You'll have to experiment with different backswing lengths to judge how far the ball travels in each situation, but that takes a single practice session, and the resulting knowledge will pay dividends for years to come. If you struggle with the technique, try raising the heel of your club. This effectively turns your iron into a putter by increasing the lie angle. With the club more upright, you'll be able to better execute the putting, stroke-type motion this shot requires.

Because the ball will be traveling on the ground, give the green a good read, and plan for the break just as you would for a putt.

THE KNOCKDOWN

To develop or improve your shot-making skills, start with the knockdown shot. This shot will teach you to make a controlled swing and to think about your options—two fundamentals all good shot-makers possess. You'll find a use for the knockdown shot in almost every round you play. I've been playing golf in Oklahoma for 70 years, and I don't remember many days when the wind wasn't blowing. The knockdown is the perfect shot for windy weather, not only when you're playing into the wind but also when you're playing downwind and need distance control. You can use this shot out of divots and other bad lies and to play underneath branches and limbs. On top of that,

The knockdown technique produces a short little swing, but one that contains plenty of power and usually a lot of spin (at least enough to expertly hold greens). The proper knockdown motion requires an arms-and-hands-dominated motion, but don't forget to continue to turn your hips through the shot. If you stop your rotation, the clubhead will sling past your hands and pull the shot way left. Plan for a lower trajectory, and be sure to experiment with a lot of different irons to get a feel for distance.

there may be days when your full swing just doesn't quite feel right. At these times, the knockdown shot can become your best friend.

You can play a knockdown shot with just about any club, even with your woods, although you do need to make certain adjustments to your setup position. Choke down a couple of inches on the grip, and take a slightly wider stance to help keep your body still during the swing (photo on top left of previous page)—the knockdown is a hands-and-arms-only shot. Play the ball back in your stance, toward your back foot. For an even lower ball flight, hood the clubface slightly (rotate it closed five to 10 degrees). The last thing you want is a shot that balloons high into the air.

After you've made these setup adjustments, simply focus on making a nice, smooth swing (photo on top right of previous page). Your lower body should stay quiet throughout, from takeaway to follow-through. Swing the club about three-quarters of the way to the top (center left photo on previous page), and be sure to stay behind the ball as you swing through impact (center right photo on previous page). You'll get a low shot that tends to curve slightly from right to left (bottom photo on previous page).

The most important element of shot-making is a positive mental outlook. If you fear the shot, you'll have trouble executing it. Another crucial element is creativity. I've seen players use a Texas wedge (a putter, for all you Northerners) from as far as 30 yards off the green. Chi Chi Rodriguez often chips with a 5 or 7 wood. Phil Mickelson has hit flop shots backward from very steep lies. These players have great imaginations—they see options other players don't.

But creativity isn't enough. The reason Rodriguez and Mickelson even attempt these shots is because they've practiced them. And practice is the only way to build confidence. Take some time at the end of each practice session to work on shot-making. If you're on the range, hit some low shots and some high ones. Play both shots to the same target to get a feel for distance control. Hit some fades and some draws. Your body will come to know what it has to do to deliver the results you want. At the short-game area, put your creative nature in overdrive. Play from bad lies, from behind and against trees, from impossible situations. No one—not even the greatest players—can execute what they haven't rehearsed.

THE LOB SHOT

Certain situations call for a high shot. You may want to hit a high shot to a tight pin or loft one over a tree. No problem. Just use a club with more loft and play the ball a little bit forward in your stance. Also, be sure to set up well behind the ball, with the majority of your weight on your right side (for a right-handed golfer). As you begin your swing, concentrate on keeping your body as quiet as possible and maintaining your weight on your right side. Don't force the shot—swinging hard will only increase the likelihood of hitting the shot thin. Remember, a high shot is generally a trouble shot. Getting the ball right down in front of the green is just fine. Again, play the shot to feed your short game.

Other situations call for an even higher shot, commonly referred to as a lob, a play in which the ball travels as high into the air as it does from you to your target. This type of shot was one of the most feared in golf—that is until the development of the lob wedge. This 60-degree wonder all but eliminated the primary fear of hitting a "lobber," or the bounce of a sand wedge bumping the leading edge of a club into the center of the golf ball.

In setting up for the flop, rotate your lob wedge slightly (remember, there's already plenty of loft built into the club), and point the leading edge at your target by rotating your body to the left. With the ball played back in your stance, hinge the club up quickly with your wrists with hardly any weight shift. From there, simply hit down and through, allowing the loft of the club to lift the ball high in the air. Relax on this shot, and make the entire swing in slow motion. You need height—not distance—on the lob. If you play it correctly, the shot will land "like a butterfly with sore feet," as the saying goes.

PUTT FROM THE FRINGE

A missed green is a missed green, even if your ball happens to wind up just a few feet from the putting surface. Good players will often find themselves in this situation, with a good lie on close-cut grass and but a few feet away from the putting surface.

A great play from here is a put. Even if there are 20 feet between you and the green, if the grass is tight, opt for the putter. Your first choice may be a wedge, but the bounce on a wedge can force the club to carom off tight lies and send the ball scurrying across the green. Plus, there's an age-old adage in golf that says it's always easier to control a ball on the ground than in the air. I believe this to be true.

The best part about this shot is that you already know how to execute it. Just be careful not to forward press too much. This will decrease the amount of loft built into the putterface and potentially force the ball to jump offline. The average putter loft is four degrees, which is needed to get the ball rolling over the grass end over end as soon as possible.

One last recommendation is to keep your normal putting grip, but to make sure not to over-hit with the right hand. This is a common error when trying to execute this shot, as many golfers believe they must hit the ball hard to get it through the grass. Simply make your normal putting stroke, with constant acceleration and easy tempo. For longer-length shots, just take the putter back a bit further, low to the ground, both back and through.

3 WOOD FROM THE FRINGE

Let's say you're near the fringe, but you have several feet of green apron to deal with. Your lie is still tight, so a wedge isn't your best chipping play, and you're certainly too far from the green to use the putter. The solution: your 3 and 5 woods. The loft of these clubs is plenty to get the ball in motion over the longer blade lengths, and their length and weight allow you to make an easy, simple motion rather than trying to pop the ball through with your putter (photos to the right). On shorter putts, use a firmer grip (for control) and simply make your standard putting motion. On longer shots (even up to 20 feet off the green), loosen your grip and make a slightly longer backswing, being careful to lead the club into the ball with the hands.

UPHILL CHIP

There are all kinds of nasty sidehill chipping situations around the green, but one of the most common is one where you're on an uphill lie. The main dangers here are popping up the ball and landing it well short of your target, or actually skulling the ball and sending it violently across the green. It's a delicate situation that demands special attention.

If you've been in this situation before, you may remember how the hill altered your perceptions and forced you to aim to the left. Hills will do that to you. That's why I'll take extra care to ensure that I've established as square a stance as possible. When I'm comfortable in my stance, I'll drop my front foot back a bit. I do this to ensure that my hips are open to the target at the finish despite the little time I'm allowed to complete the swing.

To combat hitting the ball fat, choke down on the grip. When you rest the club on the ground, keep your spine as steady as possible. I'd also recommend that you play the ball a bit back in your stance. This helps guarantee a clean hit on this awkward lie.

As far as the swing is concerned, play it much as you'd play any chip from the rough. Think of it as a swing in miniature, with a minimum of lower-body movement and a maximum of hand control.

Don't allow the slope to dictate your swing. Move the club along the target line. Also, don't make the mistake of swinging to the left in response to the hill. Practice with an eye toward hitting to where you think is right of the target. It'll be more along the line than

you think. Again, for longer shots, you can hood the face to decrease loft; on more delicate shots, open the face. Either way, be sure to extend both arms to the ball and hit down and through.

DOWNHILL BUNKER BLAST

The downhill bunker blast may be the toughest shot in golf. Before deciding on your plan of action when faced with this lie, assess your chances of success. For most golfers, the most prudent play is to work sideways out of the bunker. If you're up to the challenge, however, grab your sand wedge and heed the following keys.

Setup: Take your normal address position, then widen your stance several inches and flare your front foot open at least 45 degrees. Your body should be aimed roughly seven feet left of the target, and the ball should be played off your back foot.

Use your everyday grip, with the clubface slightly open so that the scoring lines point at your front toe. Your hands should be slightly ahead of the clubhead, with the shaft pointing at your left hip.

Adjust your shoulders to match the slope, which will steepen the plane and ensure that you hit the sand roughly two to three inches behind the ball. Your weight should slightly favor your front foot.

Backswing: First, turn your shoulders and then swing the club out. Fold your right elbow and hinge your wrists as soon as possible to create a more vertical plane.

Downswing: Make sure to maintain your wrist hinge as you start down. At impact, you want to swing down into the sand without flipping your club at the ball. This creates the proper angle of attack.

Feel: Take practice swings outside the bunker on a downhill slope with

Establish a wide stance and adjust your shoulders to match the slope.

Think steep on the way down, holding your wrist hinge as long as possible before exploding into the sand behind the ball.

the proper setup. This will help you establish the proper feel for a downhill greenside bunker shot. Feel the sand depth and texture with your feet. The firmer the sand, the farther the ball will fly. Swing shorter and softer for firm sand and longer and faster for soft sand.

Mental: Picture the ball flying out of the bunker lower than normal. If the bank in front of you is steep, plan on hitting away from the bank, even if it puts your ball farther from the hole.

Of course, this shot can be pulled off. For the greatest proof, recall tour journeyman Brian Watts and his miracle play at the 1998 British Open at Royal Birkdale. It's still the greatest bunker escape I've ever seen. Imagine a 25-footer from a greenside bunker on the 18th hole with the wind whipping off the Irish Sea and the British Open on the line. Sound too easy? Then add an awkward stance with one of your feet outside the bunker and the ball resting on a severe downslope. If you get up and down in two, you're in a playoff with a chance to win the Open—make bogey and you're out of it.

With steely nerves and flawless technique, Watts responded by pulling off what Mark O'Meara himself called "one of the greatest shots I've seen under pressure," leaving just a tap-in putt for par and a chance at golfing immortality. And although Watts (a regular on the Japan Golf Tour) eventually lost the playoff, his outstanding performance earned him $329,000 and a PGA Tour card for the 1999 season. When the Open returns to Birkdale, I'm sure they'll show the replay of this escape. Just thinking about it still sends chills down my spine.

THE 10 MOST IMPORTANT THINGS IN GOLF

8

WATCHING AND TEACHING THE GAME OF GOLF FOR THE BETTER PART OF 65 YEARS, I'VE COME TO REALIZE ONE UNIVERSAL FACT: EVERYONE SWINGS THE CLUB A DIFFERENT WAY.

Some golf swings produce better results than others, but that doesn't change the fact that the only thing your swing must do is get the ball into the hole in as few strokes as possible. This isn't to be construed as a license to move the club without thought or reason, however. Every golfer's swing needs to blend individual style with a number of swing essentials. We've gone over a lot of these so far, but when you really get down to it, there are only 10 necessities for on-course success. If you can adapt these 10 "musts" to your natural motion, you'll be primed for a lifetime of low scores.

1. USE YOUR FINGERS

Your 10 fingers are the fastest parts of your body, capable of moving more than 100 mph. As such, it's important to take full advantage of their speed. Grip the club in your fingers, not in your palms, and use your fingers to lead your swing. From takeaway to finish, think fingers and hands first; shoulders, arms, and legs are secondary. It's important not to categorize the roles of your arms, shoulders, hips, and legs as passive— they're all critical components to the overall swing motion. It's simply a matter of them playing a secondary role to your hands—the true power generators.

2. HAVE A PRESHOT ROUTINE

Not only is a preshot routine important, but so is a preround routine. Whether you're rushing from your office to make a weekday afternoon tee time or waiting on your porch for your buddy to pick you up on Saturday morning, take time to think about your forthcoming round and the things you want to accomplish. Run over some key swing thoughts, or think about how you'll attack the first hole. Often, thinking strategically about your first swing of the day will keep a poor start at bay. For every swing, pick a target and commit to it. Picture in your mind's

eye the swing you want to create and how you'll create that swing while balanced. Then, pull the trigger.

3. HAVE PRIDE

Regardless of the type of day you're having on the course, make an effort to give your game—and yourself—the respect it deserves. Often, a round in the 90s will feel more like a round in the 70s if you approach your game with an attitude that emphasizes conduct, not score. We're all going to have bad rounds and bad holes, but if you add a healthy dose of self-respect to your game, the numbers might just magically drop. Plus, how you act and perform on the course will not go unnoticed. It's easy to push aside our less-dignified moments. Others, however, won't be so lenient, and you never want to be "that guy" or "that gal" around any course.

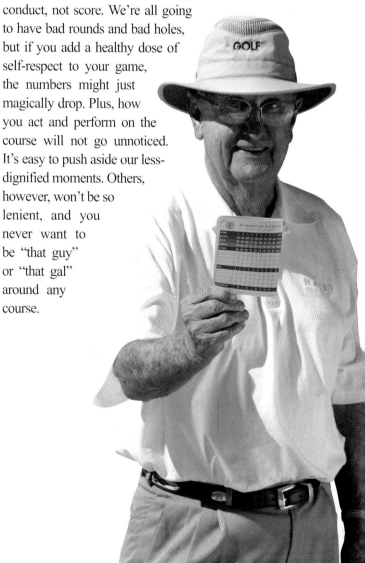

4. STAY IN BALANCE

It's not very often you fall down while standing on a street corner, but people often do that very thing while swinging the club. That's because they're not balanced. Adopt a stance that mimics the one you use in everyday life: not too narrow (which facilitates too much turn and the chance to reverse pivot) or too wide (which limits your ability to coil). Make it natural.

5. DROP THE CLUB

It's the most difficult thing to master in golf, but unfortunately, dropping the club to start the downswing is an absolute necessity to move the club with power and on the desired inside-out path. What's more damaging than not dropping the hands and club is what you'll likely do instead, which is starting the club back down with a lunge forward or an early release of the hands. From the top, allow your hands simply to fall toward the ground. Combine that with a gradual turn toward the target, and you'll naturally shift your weight to your left side and guard against the dreaded pull and pull slice.

6. SPIN THE TOP

One of my favorite images to describe the golf swing is a top. Remember those? In order to get the top to spin as fast as possible, you had to wrap the string around the top as tightly as you could. Same goes in the golf swing, where your club is the top and your body is the string and your main goal is to coil your body as much as your flexibility allows (see chapter 3 for more information). The best way to do this is to dominate your backswing with a strong turn of the shoulders while minimizing your hip turn (photos at right). The key: set your left knee as an anchor and your right knee as a hub around which everything turns. Now, you're coiled.

7. SET UP FOR SUCCESS

We've already dedicated several pages of this book to the setup, and guess what? Here's more, which should speak volumes about how critical it is to address a golf ball correctly. At the very least, a proper setup can—and will—greatly reduce the chance of golf's most common malignancy: the slice.

A. THE KEYS TO A SOLID ADDRESS INCLUDE TILTING YOUR SPINE SLIGHTLY AWAY FROM THE TARGET SO YOUR LEFT SHOULDER SITS HIGHER THAN YOUR RIGHT, ABOUT AS MUCH AS YOUR RIGHT HAND SITS BELOW YOUR LEFT ON THE GRIP. ANGLING THE SPINE BETTER ALLOWS YOU TO SWING THE CLUB FROM INSIDE OUT. YOUR HEAD TILT SHOULD MIMIC YOUR SPINE TILT, AS WELL.

B. A MISTAKE MANY GOLFERS MAKE IS SETTING UP WITH OPEN SHOULDERS, AN ERROR FUELED BY THE DESIRE TO HIT HARD WITH THE RIGHT SIDE. DON'T FALL INTO THAT TRAP. INSTEAD, PLAY THE BALL A BIT BACK IN YOUR STANCE, POSITION YOUR HEAD SLIGHTLY BEHIND THE BALL, AND KEEP THAT RIGHT ELBOW LOOSE AND ON YOUR RIGHT HIP. THESE SETUP KEYS WILL HELP YOU KEEP YOUR SHOULDERS FROM OPENING, A MALADY THAT, MORE OFTEN THAN NOT, WILL CREATE A SLICE SWING.

C. I RECOMMEND A SHOULDER-WIDTH STANCE WITH YOUR FEET FLARED. IF YOU DON'T FLARE YOUR FEET, YOU'LL MAKE IT MORE DIFFICULT TO EXECUTE A BIG TURN OF THE SHOULDERS ON THE BACKSWING. FURTHERMORE, WITH A FLARED FRONT FOOT, YOU'LL ENCOURAGE A MORE EFFICIENT TRANSFER OF WEIGHT TO YOUR FRONT SIDE ON THE DOWNSWING. AS FAR AS BALL POSITION IS CONCERNED, PLAY THE BALL OFF THE LOGO OF YOUR SHIRT. PLAYING THE BALL TOO FAR FORWARD MAY ENCOURAGE PULLS AND PULL SLICES.

8. GET THE CLUB UP

The golf swing has two parts: the "around" and the "up and down." Most recreational players can execute both parts, but rarely can they blend the two together. Think turn first: with your hands leading the way, simply turn your shoulders to get the club to the top. As you do so, imagine placing the clubshaft over your right shoulder while, at the same time, focusing on keeping your hands as far away from your head as possible. This thought establishes the "up" part of your backswing. On the way to your finish, do the same thing: keep your turn going and strive to get that clubshaft above your shoulder, this time the left one. Combine these moves with a shallow arc through impact, and you'll find extra power and accuracy.

9. FINISH LOW

One of my favorite sayings is, "In golf, you shake hands like a gentleman; you never high-five." In other words, through impact, keep your hands low to the ground instead of lifting them high into the air. If you try to finish low, you'll encourage a better forward weight shift and crisper ball-striking. Plus, it's absolutely critical that, when you strike the ball with a descending blow when swinging your irons and wedges, you produce a nice, healthy divot after the golf ball. (Don't confuse this with a driver swing, however. A driver should ascend through the contact area.) Hit down and through, and keep the hands low in your release until you move to your finish. If you "high-five," or move from low to high in your release, you'll run the risk of topping the ball and encourage a fade or push ball flight.

10. KEEP YOUR HEAD BACK

Although it's likely that you've never placed yours on a scale, the average human head weighs about 14 pounds, which is a significant amount of weight. If that weight moves too far forward on the downswing,

it will throw your entire motion out of balance. As you swing back to the ball, make a conscious effort to keep your head back toward your right foot. This encourages a more powerful release. As you keep your head back, don't forget to turn. Allow that right shoulder to continue its rotation toward the target. When you feel your shoulder approach your chin, allow your head to turn with it.

The above sequence of photographs of Lee Trevino shows exactly what I'm talking about. At address, notice the bill of Trevino's cap—it's well behind his tee. Now, watch his head throughout his backswing to the top position. His head is moved even further back (though he's turned within the confines of his right hip). In the downswing sequence, Trevino's power just jumps off the page, but guess what? His head never changes its position. It merely rotates with his shoulders so that, in the release, he's watching the ball along the target line. With a swing like this, and the ability to hang back with the best of them, it's no wonder Trevino was feared throughout his entire career.

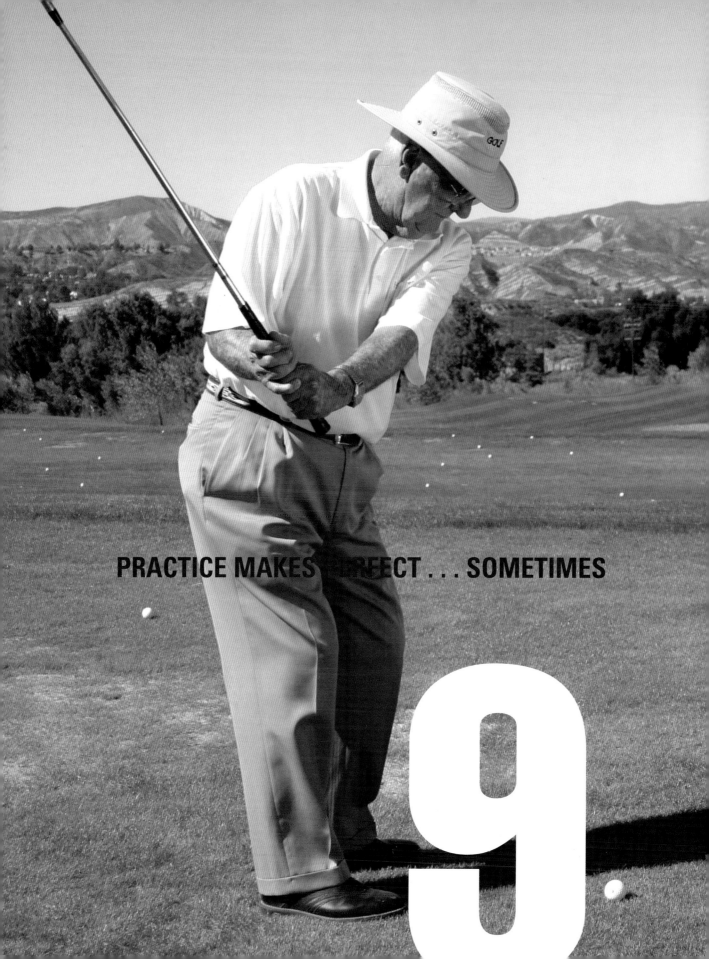

PRACTICE MAKES PERFECT . . . SOMETIMES

9.

WE'VE JUST FINISHED GOING OVER SOME LESSONS
THAT CAN MAKE A REAL DIFFERENCE IN YOUR GOLF GAME—IF YOU CAN BRING THEM TO THE GOLF COURSE.

That's where practice comes in. People will tell you that practice makes perfect. I'll tell you that this old saying isn't always true when it comes to golf. Good practice makes improvement. That's what I emphasize. You practice in order to hone skills that you can use on the golf course. That means you have to treat practice with the same seriousness and high regard that you treat a round of golf.

I think practicing is one of the most misunderstood parts of golf. Think of how often you've heard a friend—or maybe even yourself—say, "I'm going out to hit some balls." Show me a golfer who goes to the range to "hit some balls," and I'll show you a golfer who won't ever get it right on the course. That's because he or she hasn't learned the right way to practice.

I've been lucky. When I was young, my good friend George Coleman had a visitor from Texas come stay with him in my hometown of Miami, Oklahoma. The friend was one of his fellow professionals, a small, quiet man named Ben Hogan. You can make the argument that Ben Hogan was one of the best golfers ever to play the game. But there's no doubt that he was the very best when it came to practice.

Hogan practiced with the same famous intensity he showed on the course. He was hard on himself, a perfectionist who judged every shot—even on the range—as though his career hung on its outcome.

"Mr. Hogan," someone once asked, "when you're practicing, how often are you working on something specific, and how often are you simply grooving your swing?"

Hogan answered with a characteristic snort, "I'm always working on something specific," he said, "or I wouldn't be here."

On several occasions in 1947 I got to shag balls for Hogan. Almost 60 years later, I can still see those shots coming at me. It's a shame that kids don't get the chance to shag balls these days. There's no better way to learn about shot-making than to see it from the receiving end. Driving ranges have become big business, and automatic ball-pickers have ended the great tradition of shagging balls, just like golf carts have all but done away with caddies. But I'll never forget what it was like to be stationed at exactly 145 or 163 or 187 yards from Hogan and his mountain of golf balls. And when I say exactly, I mean it. If I had to take a step forward or back to catch the shot, Hogan would shake his head in disgust—not at the inaccuracy of his ball-striking, but at the inaccuracy of my paces. The thing I'll always remember is the shape of those shots. He would hit high ones that I'd play like pop flies. Then he'd hit low ones that came screaming at my mitt like extra-base line drives. He'd bend shots from right to left, then from left to right. And never did I have to move to field the ball. I can't tell you how much I learned on those hot afternoons. It's one thing to stand on the tee firing shots at a pin. It's quite another to be the pin.

Of the many lessons I learned from Hogan's practice technique, the one that has stuck with me the longest, as player and teacher, is his devotion to precision. He was never trying to see how far he could hit the ball. Instead, he was always trying to hit it exactly so far. Whether it was a driver, a wedge, a 5 iron—it didn't matter. The object was to hit the precise shot he imagined. Anything less was failure. In other words, Ben Hogan never once went to the practice range to "hit balls." He was there to hit shots. I suggest you take a cue from the master on that point.

How much should you practice? That's a personal choice. I've known players who would practice four times a week and play only once. That seems a little backward to me, but then I've always enjoyed playing golf more than practicing. I guess the only real guideline is that you should practice enough to show improvement on the course. If you spend your practice time wisely—rehearsing for the shots you'll have to hit when you play—you'll find that you don't need endless hours of range work. If you just go out and start swinging away on the practice tee, then no amount of work will be enough. It will never result in lower scores.

If you want to improve your play through practice, you're going to have to make your practice work for you.

FOCUS ON THE SHORT GAME

The biggest problem people have with practicing is that they've got the percentages all wrong. They go out and hit hundreds of full shots and totally ignore the most important part of scoring—the short game. We've all seen so-called short-game magicians. Seve Ballesteros is one. So is Tom Kite. You probably know someone at your home course who never seems to have a horrible score, even when he's hitting it badly. Don't think that these guys were just born with great imagination and soft hands. I know better. I've seen some of the greatest short-game players of all time, and I'll tell you this: not a single one of them was born with it. They had to develop their skills the old-fashioned way, by practicing. This is good news for you.

Gary Player is the greatest bunker player of all time. A lot of golfers know that. What they don't know is that Player used to go into the practice bunker every day and not leave until he had holed out a shot. If he holed out the first one, that was it. But if it took eight hours, he would stay in there until a shot found the cup. The point of this story is that every time he hit a practice shot, he was trying to make it. That carried over into his on-course game, and the rest is history. In other words, he practiced with on-course performance in mind, and it paid off.

The fact is that more than half of the shots you hit on the course measure 60 yards or less. Knowing what to do around the greens can wash away many of the sins your full swing commits. It's just a simple matter of math that you should spend about 70 to 75 percent of your practice time on pitching, chipping, bunker play, and putting. This is the fastest way to see practice make a difference in your scores.

IT'S ALL IN THE MIX

The short game is all about distance control and understanding how the ball will behave after it's on the green. You can hit high lob shots that hardly run at all, or you can go for low shots that spend most of their time rolling. Practicing the short game is the only way to get a feel for proper shot selection, and that's what lets you save strokes. Stand in the same place with five balls and hit five different shots to the same target. What are the advantages or disadvantages of each? Your opponents may start talking about your imagination on the course. You'll know it's just plain old common sense.

On the course, no two short shots are alike. That's the way it should be in your practice sessions as well. You need to practice all types of shots from all types of lies. Work your way around the practice green in a big circle, hitting a few shots from 20, 10, and 5 yards from the green's edge. Work off of downhill, sidehill, and uphill lies, and make a mental note of how your stance and lie affect the shot. When you go into the bunker, practice shots from good lies, from footprints, from rake grooves, etc. Bury balls up under the lip, and figure out the most effective way to get out. Practice long shots and short ones.

The goal of short-game practice is to eliminate surprises on the course. Major league batters know that a pitcher is most effective during his first rotation through the order. After that, you've seen his windup, his delivery, and the movement of the pitches. There are no more surprises the second time around, and the hitters begin to feel more comfortable. Your short-game practice should let you know what kinds of shots the course can throw at you. If you've seen it before, it's just not as intimidating.

A LITTLE HELP FROM YOUR FRIENDS

The best thing you can do for short-game practice is to invite a friend to join you. I used to get into tremendous practice green games with former PGA Tour player Woody Blackburn. We would challenge each other at $1 per shot; the winner of the last shot got to pick the next. We ended up playing all types of up-and-down shots—over hedges and trees, under branches, shots that had to roll through bunkers—you name it. And there's no better putting practice than playing small-stakes games on the putting green. What I love about this kind of competitive practicing is that it helps you keep your focus and teaches you to deal with the pressure you're sure to encounter when you're playing. And there's nothing better than sticking it to a friend, even if it's just for some tees or a soda. Practice that stokes your competitive fire is practice that will stay with you for a long, long time—especially if it's practice that teaches you how to save strokes.

HOME ON THE RANGE

I'm not against full-swing practice. You need it in order to become a better ball striker. What I'm against is the idea of going out just to pound balls into a wide-open driving range. Practice is a discipline. There's no other word for it. In many areas of life today, discipline is in short supply. But if you want to improve your golf game and put yourself in a better position to enjoy all the benefits this great game can deliver, discipline is key. There's an old Chinese saying: "A mule is good if tamed, but he who tames himself is better." That's what practicing is all about: taming yourself. That's why you need to have a consistent and manageable practice routine.

A good practice routine helps you focus on the session and block out other distractions. One of my favorite photographs shows a golfer intently practicing on the range while the clubhouse is literally in flames behind him. The message is clear—his practice routine had begun, and nothing was going to snap him out of it.

Your practice session should always begin with goal setting. What do you plan to carry away from the range on that particular day? Write it down before you begin. Be specific with both your long game and short game. For instance, you may want to work on drawing the ball with your mid-irons. Or you may want to work on trajectory—producing a higher or lower ball flight. Maybe you've been struggling with the soft lob shot. Don't set goals that you can't achieve. If you consistently hit a severe left-to-right banana ball, you're not going to start drawing it in one session. In that case you might want to focus on turning that sharp slice into a fade that you can play. Regardless of the lesson, always have goals and commit to them.

When your goals for the session are clear, take the time to warm up properly so that your body and mind are ready to get down to business. Start by selecting your practice location. By that I mean where on the range you are going to work. I have my students work at one end of the range, as far away from other people as possible. The range is no place for socializing. You want to be able to concentrate and work, like an artist in a studio.

Start with your sand wedge and hit a few 20-yard shots. Work on making simple swings, feeling your hands and arms working while minimizing body movement. When you're comfortable at 20 yards, move to 50-yard shots. Hit a few of those, again making nice, even-tempo swings and concentrating on solid contact in the middle of the clubface. Think about rhythm—back and through. Point your thumb to heaven on the backswing, and shake hands with your friend on the follow-through.

If the range is busy and you can't actually pace off your shots, you should at least pace off the distance between measurement plates and the tee markers. Your practice sessions should leave you knowing exactly how far you hit each club, from your lob wedge to your driver. If you get nothing out of practice except that knowledge, then you've spent your time wisely.

THE ONLY DRILLS YOU'LL EVER NEED

A lot of players—from amateurs to touring pros—have asked me for drills they can use on the range. I'm not a big believer in complex drills.

Most of the time you can't use them on the golf course anyway. But there are a couple of drills that I like to incorporate into every practice session, usually after I've finished working through all my clubs. The first is the half-swing drill. Take 20 balls and hit them using only half swings. The club should point up to the sky on the backswing and up to the sky again on the follow-through.

The second drill is similar to the first, but adds to it. This is the one-club, many-targets drill. Take a club, say a 7 iron, and hit five balls to a target at a normal 7-iron distance (approximately 150 yards for most golfers). Then hit five balls to a target 10 yards nearer than the first. Then hit five more balls to a target another 10 yards nearer, all the way down to 100 yards. This teaches you to scale your swing while maintaining good rhythm. Work on staying behind the ball and accelerating through the shot, regardless of how long it is. Both of these drills help you to focus on hitting the ball squarely while making nice, controlled swings.

AND A SURPRISE ENDING FOR YOUR RANGE SESSION

You've now constructed a good practice routine, but your range session isn't quite finished yet. With the last 10 balls of the day, I want you to think back to the most difficult, awkward, full shots you faced the last time you played. You may have had to hit a ball under low-hanging branches, or you may have needed to bend a shot around a tree or into a crosswind. You may have encountered a shot off hardpan or out of a divot. The hardest shots to hit are the ones you've never tried. And again, if the goal of practice is to improve your on-course play, then you need to keep the course at the front of your mind during practice. Ending your session this way will help. Recall those difficult shots and re-create them on the range. Hit each of the shots five times, experimenting to gain a feel for what will be successful in dealing with the situations. These are lessons that you give yourself. Soon enough, you will come to understand that your own practice may be the greatest teacher of all.

PRACTICING ON THE GOLF COURSE

You play golf on the golf course, not on the driving range. So the best place to practice is obviously on the course itself, right? The range can be a good substitute, but you should never pass up the opportunity to get some of what I call "live" practice. Try to get out in the early morning or late afternoon, when you will not be slowing traffic or disturbing other players. Even three or four holes of on-course practice can be a real boost for your game.

My favorite way to practice on the course is to play two balls. Play each hole two different ways. On a dogleg, you may want to play one ball with a driver, cutting off distance and going for birdie. Take the conservative route with the other ball. You'll soon get a feeling for percentages and for the style that makes you the most comfortable.

Another great practice game is to tee off on every hole with a 5 iron. That way, you'll end up hitting approach shots with clubs you would never normally hit. Anything that can extend and challenge your comfort zone is good for your game. If you've had trouble with a certain hole on your home course because you tend to miss the ball to the right, spend some time in your trouble spot. Practice different escape shots from different positions in the right rough so that you'll be prepared the next time you're forced to play out of that area. Then go back and try to play the hole a different way, with another iron off the tee, for instance. You just might find that you've been trying to force a square peg into a round hole, rather than playing to your strengths. Those kinds of discoveries are what good practice is all about.

Think about this question: what have your most recent five practice sessions taught you about your game? If you have trouble coming up with an answer, you need to overhaul your practice strategy.

THE ART OF COMPETING

People play golf for many reasons. But I've never bought into the idea of playing golf purely for relaxation. Deep down inside, the game of golf nurtures a competitive spirit. No other sport offers as many competitive possibilities, whether we're talking about friendly wagers with your buddies or national championships. Vince Lombardi was wrong when he said that winning was the "only thing." It's the competition itself that makes you feel alive. Golf is not about proving anything to anyone else. It's about proving something to yourself. That's why competition is so important.

When you reach down inside and find that there's something there, you know that your hard work has paid off. On those occasions when you lose, you learn even more about yourself and your game. In order to develop a competitive game, you need discipline, patience, faith, and a good work ethic. Is it any surprise that a person who displays these traits on the golf course often achieves success in his or her other endeavors as well?

So many golfers ask me how they'll know when they're ready for competition. I believe that you're ready as soon as you start thinking about it. Competition gives you so many opportunities to learn and achieve and to meet other people who love golf and love the thrill of testing their games against their nerves. Go for it.

OVER-PRACTICING

If there's one mistake I see in golfers who are new to competition or who compete too infrequently, it's that they over-practice. Rather than staying in their normal rhythm, they start "preparing" weeks in advance. Competition is an extension of your game, not something totally different. If you tend to play rather than practice heavily, why on earth would you suddenly start going to the driving range two weeks before a tournament? That's going to get you out of your rhythm.

Dr. Gil Morgan is one of the finest golfers the state of Oklahoma has ever produced. I can't even remember a time that I've seen him on the practice tee if it wasn't just to loosen up before a round. Gil is a player, not a practicer. The most famous nonpracticer on the PGA Tour is Bruce Lietzke. His caddie once claimed to have put a banana under the headcover of Lietzke's driver at the end of a tournament. Lietzke then took one of his frequent long breaks from the tour. Six weeks later, at the end of the break, the caddie pulled the headcover off of the driver as they were about to warm up for the first round. The banana was still there, although it was in much worse shape after the layoff than Bruce's swing was.

I've known only a handful of players who had the talent to base their games on mechanics. Ben Hogan was one of them. Tom Kite is another. Kite uses practice as a meditation, a way to clear his mind. He relies on confidence in his mechanics, and he needs a lot of practice time as a result. But he has a tremendous understanding of the golf swing, which is hard to develop if you haven't spent an entire lifetime at it. Nick Faldo tried for years to base his game on mechanics, but I think it hurt him as much as it helped him. You have to be able to win even when your swing is a little off.

The message here is that there is no right or wrong way for you to get ready for competition. But there is a right way and a wrong way for you to prepare. Your challenge is to recognize what works for you and to have the faith to stick with it. If you're playing well, you're preparing well. If not, try a different way of getting ready.

One of the easiest ways to tell if you're preparing properly is to look at the way you play the first few holes of your competitive rounds. Do you tend to get uptight on the first tee and make mistakes on the early holes? If you do, it's probably because you have been practicing too much or warming up too much before the round. After a few holes, you forget about all the mechanical thoughts you tried to transfer from the range, and you settle into a better frame of mind.

Most players would do much better to spend more practice time on their short games and on the putting green. Ball-striking comes and goes, no matter how much you practice. When you focus on your short game, you learn to focus on saving strokes. That's what helps you lower your scores. Remember this: a good short game will bail you out of poorly struck shots much better than well-struck shots will make up for a poor short game.

NERVES

I'll just tell you right now that any player who tells you he's not nervous on the first tee of a big tournament or important round is lying. Maybe they don't mean to lie, but the simple truth is that you can't help getting nervous when you feel as though you have something to prove. The pressure only increases if you play well for the first rounds of a tournament. And the sad fact is that sometimes you'll fail, no matter who you are. Who will ever forget that painful Sunday when Greg Norman, after three days of flawless golf, let The Masters championship he wanted so badly slip away? There was no explanation for his final-round 78 other than nerves.

Tom Watson is one of the greatest winners of all time. In his prime, it was very rare for him to succumb to the pressure. But it wasn't always that way. Watson first appeared on the professional scene at the 1974 U.S. Open at Winged Foot Golf Club. Against a tough field and an even tougher golf course, the young pro held the lead after 54 holes and spent a fitful night tossing and turning and dreaming of being U.S. Open champion. The next day he shot 79. The following year he again held the lead after 54 holes, and again he folded. But later in that summer of 1975, Watson won his first PGA Tour event, the Western Open. Then he won the British Open. For the next decade he was the dominant player in golf.

What turned Watson from a choker into a champion? He learned to stop complicating his game with visions of things he couldn't control—like victories. Instead, he learned to maintain his focus and concentrate simply on playing a good round of golf. He developed a strong sense of faith that if he just played well, the rest would take care of itself. And it did, time and time again.

The great winners rarely talk about winning. Instead, they talk about the thrill of being in the hunt. Winners thrive on the nerves that build as they close in on the final few holes of a tournament. The players who consistently fall a shot short fear those same nerves. Winners know that losing is just a step in their education. Losers fear that they will always be branded a loser if they fail. You can't avoid getting nervous on the golf course. Who would want to? Getting nervous means you've played yourself into position to achieve a goal. Have you ever stood on the final tee knowing that you needed a par for a personal-best score? Tell me your hands weren't shaking. It's no coincidence that the first place you feel your nerves is in your hands. So that's where to start when finding the best way to deal with the pressure.

Your instinct when you get nervous is to tighten up. When you tighten up on the golf club, all sorts of bad things can happen. Try this: next time you find yourself getting nervous, whether you're on the first tee of a big match or coming down the stretch with a chance to set a personal best or win a tournament, shake out your hands. Go on and shake them out like a swimmer getting ready for the start of a race. Flick your fingers in a 1-2-3-4 rhythm. Now take three deep breaths, and go through your regular preshot routine. Don't worry about the result. You've already achieved something simply by playing into a position to get nervous. There is no failure from here, only experience.

PATIENCE

Competitive golf is a lot like prizefighting. The last one left standing is often the one who wins. This means you have to be patient and prevent isolated mistakes from piling up on each other. Most of all, you have to accept that you can't force something to happen. You have to be patient.

Curtis Strange has enjoyed a long career at the top levels of competitive golf. His greatest moment came when he won the 1989 U.S. Open at Oak Hill Country Club in Rochester, New York, to become the first person since Hogan to successfully defend his title. In professional golf, the name of the game is usually birdies. But when you throw in a healthy dose of thick rough, fast greens, and U.S. Open pressure, everything changes. Although Strange had, at times, shown a great deal of impatience with his golf game, this day was different. He started out three shots behind leader Kite. But rather than coming out firing at the pins and trying to make up those shots quickly, he began with a methodical string of pars and just kept adding to it. All of a sudden Kite, who was struggling with the pressure of trying to win his first major championship, hit a wild tee shot and made triple bogey. Now Strange was tied for the lead. The pars just kept coming. He missed a few birdie chances—some that he should have made. But he didn't allow himself to get aggressive. He just kept making pars. Soon he had played the front nine in all pars. Then he made par on the first six holes on the back nine. Then, on the difficult 16th hole, a 25-foot birdie putt found the cup almost by accident. That one birdie was all he needed. He finished his round with pars on 17 and 18 and raised his arms in victory.

Later, when someone asked him what his mindset was for that day, Strange said, "I just tried to par the golf course to death."

LEARNING A GOLF COURSE

If you play a golf course enough times, eventually you learn how to score on it. You instinctively play away from trouble spots. You know where the scoring opportunities are and where disaster lurks. You know how the greens break and how the ball bounces. You know how the course plays when it's wet and how it plays when it's dry.

But when you're preparing for a competition, you'll be lucky to get one or two chances to see the golf course. That means you've got to learn it quickly. Your best shot at seeing how the course plays is your practice round.

Don't worry about your score during a practice round. You have to remember that the purpose of the round is education, not excellence. You'll use the information you gain during the practice round for your mental rehearsals and on-course decisions throughout the week. The idea is to learn as much about the course as possible.

Make notes on positioning off the tee box. Which holes are good driver holes? Where should you hit an iron in order to lay up at your favorite distance for a good approach opportunity? You can't overpower a golf course, especially one that you haven't played many times. Start conservatively, and as you learn more about the course throughout the tournament, you can refine your game plan off the tee.

The real benefit of local knowledge of a golf course comes on and around the greens, and this is where you want to spend the most time during the practice round. Study the contours and shapes on the greens.

Where would the good pin positions be? Take a look at the penalties for missing the green short, to the sides, and long. Which areas give you the best chances to get up and down?

Does the course play long and soft, or is it hard and fast? You have to know this so that you can practice the appropriate wedge shots and chips. On a wet course where there's not much run, you'll need to gear your short game to higher shots that fly most of the way to the pin. On a fast course, you may want to practice your Texas wedge shots and other bump and runs. Take as many notes as you can, and review them later. If you take away the element of surprise from a golf course, you've taken away its greatest weapon. By playing a smart practice round, you'll be able to recognize a sucker pin before you've become the sucker. You can always recover from a bogey, but doubles hurt.

After your practice round, go directly to the short-game area and, using your notes, work on the shots you'll need on the course. Imagine yourself playing specific shots to specific greens. Your mind doesn't know the difference between rehearsing on the practice green and rehearsing on the golf course. It just feels more prepared because of the rehearsal.

PLAY YOUR GAME, PLAY TO WIN

After the tournament begins, you need to trust in your game and yourself. The routines that work for you in friendly rounds with your buddies will work in tournament play, too. The key is to eliminate the dumb mistakes and to let everything else take care of itself. Enjoy the fellowship of other serious players. Every time you play a competitive round, you're learning. You'll learn about the strengths and weaknesses of your own game, and you'll learn from the other players in the event. Over time, competition will improve your game more than a thousand hours on the practice tee ever could.

Add competition into every round you play. Don't create life-or-death situations, but always give yourself a prize to play for, whether it's a few bucks with your friends or something for yourself if you break a personal record on the course.

A golf writer I know was talking recently about an article he'd seen where a number of other golf writers were listing the greatest moments in golf. Most of them were picking Hogan's 1951 U.S. Open victory, Jack Nicklaus' 1986 Masters win, and other high-profile victories by the game's top players. But my friend had a different take. He told me how he had gone out for nine holes at his local course one evening and was paired with two women. On the 7th tee, one of the women turned to him and said that it looked like she had a chance to break 60, on nine holes, for the first time.

"I've always said I'd treat myself to an expensive day at a spa if I did it," she said.

By the time they reached the 9th tee, it had become quite dark. The woman squinted at her scorecard and said that she needed a 7 on the 9th, a tough par-4 with water down the right side, to achieve her goal. Her drive was a good one, down the fairway. Her second shot sounded good, but it flew into the darkness. After a few minutes of searching, she declared that it must have gone in the water.

"Well," my friend said, "that's tough to say. I think we could let you drop another one."

She shook her head. "No, I hit it at the water. I have to say that it went in."

She dropped her third and then duffed her fourth shot. With the tension rising and the darkness increasing, she duffed her fifth shot, too. The sixth shot was better, but it came to rest at the front of the green, some 40 feet from the hole. Then, with my friend tending the flagstick, she rolled that 40-footer dead center into the cup for her 7.

"I still get chills thinking about it," my friend confesses.

The woman leapt in the air, gave high-fives to her partner and my friend, and let out a whoop that lit up the night.

"I've seen a lot of great moments in golf," my friend told me, "but never one any better than that."

That woman had won a major victory. She met adversity head-on, emerged with her sense of honor intact, and pulled a little miracle up from deep inside.

Now if that's not winning, I just don't know what is.

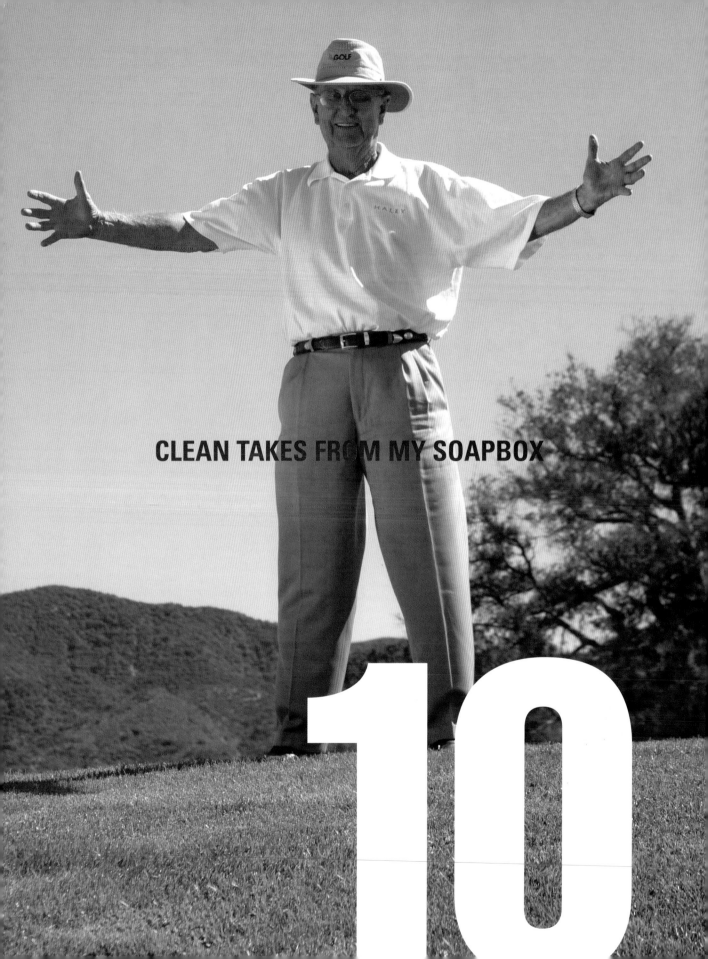

CLEAN TAKES FROM MY SOAPBOX

10

MAKE NO MISTAKE, THE GAME OF GOLF IS ITS OWN SOCIETY, AND LIKE EVERY SOCIETY, THERE ARE LAWS AND ETHICS.

As we all know, our laws are often broken, and ethics—well, let's just say that sometimes they take a backseat to the pressures of succeeding in our modern world.

I like to believe that golf is above all that. Our game is for gentlemen and ladies. Now you may think that sounds old-fashioned, but I'll tell you that old-fashioned isn't so bad when it comes to treating each other right. Golf is a tie that binds us together, and if we want to keep it that way, etiquette and the *Rules of Golf* are the best places to start.

I can't tell you how to lead your life—except when you step on a golf course. In eight decades, I've seen it all, and I strongly believe that I know what's best for this game and for you as a golfer. Plus, it's my book, and I'm ready to get on my soapbox. Don't worry—it's for your own good.

MAKE ETIQUETTE THE MOST IMPORTANT RULE

I've worked with thousands of golfers during my life. And while the lessons vary, every player with whom I work comes out of our sessions knowing the etiquette of golf. I've always believed in the Golden Rule—do unto others as you would have them do unto you. That's etiquette in a nutshell.

You wouldn't want to eat dinner with someone who chewed with his or her mouth open or clanged silverware loudly on the dishes throughout the meal. And you wouldn't want to play golf with someone who showed no consideration for you and your game. Golf is going to give you chances to get to know people who can change your life. Don't mess it up by being sloppy on the course and making the day a frustrating experience.

Etiquette begins on the first tee. Greet all the players in your group with a firm handshake and wish them luck. Make sure you know everybody's name. You're getting ready to spend four hours of your life with these folks. Why would you want to treat them like strangers? If I'm playing with new people, I make a note on my scorecard so I can remember their names. The winners in business never forget names. Neither do the winners in golf.

Almost everyone knows to be quiet when another player is swinging. But you should take it one step further: give each player a chance to prepare for each shot in silence. I'd rather have you talking during my backswing than yammering on while I'm going through my preshot routine. That's the source of your concentration.

Stand clear of a player's line during his or her shot. Don't forget that the line runs not only from the ball to the hole, but back from the ball and well past the hole as well. Position yourself out of the player's view by standing still, well off to the side.

Keep your hands out of your pockets while the other players in your group are playing their shots. It's easy to get "rabbit ears" on the golf course, where you hear almost everything. Sam Snead's putting difficulties are legendary. To perform on the greens, he needed all the concentration he could muster. During one tournament, a lady following Snead's group was carrying coins in her pocket. As she stood off to the side of the green, she would absentmindedly jingle the coins with her hand. She never meant to distract anyone, but the constant rattle at every green drove Snead crazy. Finally, Snead found a solution. After holing out, he went and found the woman in the gallery.

"Ma'am," he said, fishing a dollar bill out of his own pocket, "do you have change for a dollar?"

The key to practicing good etiquette is just to stay aware. Know where your shadow falls, and try to keep it out of your fellow player's line of sight. If you realize that you don't have time to move before they play, stay still. It's not too much trouble to play through a shadow, but one that's moving can be a real annoyance.

Don't step in a player's line when you're on the green. You may not even leave a mark on the green, but you'll surely make an impression in the minds of the other golfers in your group. Failing to pay attention to the games of your partners is just as much a breach of etiquette as purposely interfering is.

HURRY UP AND MISS IT

The most common etiquette violation in golf is slow play. You don't play better golf by taking longer to do it, and you don't have to rush to play at a good pace. Playing at a good pace is a courtesy that extends to the groups in front of you and behind you—and to everybody on the golf course during your round.

Too many people confuse bad play with slow play. I've known plenty of bad golfers who never held up play on a golf course. They're more conscious of playing slowly than just about anyone else. The worst slow-play culprits are often the better players. They're the ones who fidget and fuss the most. The PGA Tour is a swamp of slow play. Now, I admire Jack Nicklaus for everything he's accomplished in golf, but he is the worst slow player in the history of the game. He's not alone, of course. If golf courses were made of wet cement, Bernhard Langer, Nick Faldo, and Tiger Woods would be statues by now.

I learned long ago that there's no excuse for a good player to be a slow player. The most telling lesson came from my good friend George Coleman. Coleman was a native of my hometown who went on to great things in business and in golf. He won the Oklahoma State Amateur Championship in the 1930s. He traveled with Ky Laffoon on many road trips and met Bing Crosby, Bob Hope, and a young Texan named Ben Hogan. Whether in the boardroom or on the golf course, Coleman always made sure he treated people right. The most prestigious clubs in America sought him out as a member. He belonged to Augusta National and was president of Seminole Golf Course and Club in Florida for many years. Their invitational tournament is named in his honor.

Coleman detested slow play. He was a busy man, and he saw time wasted as time lost. The last thing he wanted to do was stand around waiting for someone to get ready to play. When it was his turn to play, he already had his glove on, knew his distance, and had his club selected. "If you're gonna miss it," he said to me more than once, "just hurry up and miss it. I don't have all day."

I have never forgotten that.

BE READY

You hear so much these days about playing "ready golf," where the person ready to hit goes ahead and plays, regardless of the honor or the position of his ball. I'll tell you now that I'm not a big fan of ready golf. Using the honor on the tee box and the traditional order of play through the green is a great part of the game. But that doesn't mean you can't play quickly. The key is to be ready when it's your turn.

Although there are a thousand instructors out there who might tell you otherwise, there's not much science to hitting a golf ball. Figure your yardage, select your club, and play the shot. Your routine should be well under way while the other members of your group are playing their shots. Don't wait until your turn rolls around to start pulling your glove out of your pocket and start pacing yardages.

Being ready means being ready to move to the next hole as well. When you get to the green, do everyone on the course a favor and leave your cart or bag between the green and the next tee. Making the next group wait while you go all the way back across the green after holing out is a sure way to make enemies.

Finally, pick up your ball if you're out of the hole (except in tournament play, of course). Some courses have a double-par rule, which means when you get to eight shots on a par-4 and still haven't holed out, pick up the ball. I say that should be the absolute latest you pick up the ball. Everybody struggles on a hole every now and then. If you have a handicap, you have certain maximum scores you can take. When you reach them, put the ball in your pocket, and concentrate on doing better on the next hole.

THE ART OF PLAYING THROUGH

No matter how quickly you play, there will always be groups who play even faster. I have a neighbor and business partner who is a member of the beautiful Bighorn Golf Club in Palm Desert, California. It was there that I saw the fastest group of golfers I've ever seen. The owner of the Bighorn development loves golf, but even more than that, he loves high-speed golf. I've seen him only once, and that was all it took for me to know I'd never see a faster player.

We were on the 10th hole, and our forecaddie waved me over to the side of the fairway. "That's the owner and his group back on the tee," the caddie said. "You might as well let them play through."

We waved them through and waited for them to motor down the fairway to play their approach shots. Before we even knew it, they had jumped out of their carts, hit the balls, and were nothing but four backs disappearing down the fairway in souped-up golf carts.

"How do they stand?" our caddie asked the owner's forecaddie as we stood off to the side.

"Fifty-five minutes to here. They're taking it easy today."

Now I don't believe that golf should be a race. My point is only that there will be times when you just have to let another group play through, so you might as well know how to do it properly. Otherwise, you'll botch up the flow of the entire golf course. At Bighorn it was easy because there was no one else around. That won't be the case most of the time.

Playing through or having another group play through is a last resort. Don't do it until you've made every effort to pick up your pace. If you're keeping pace with the group in front of you, don't worry about being pushed from behind—there's nowhere you can go. But if you do have to let someone through, it's a lot easier if you know what you're doing.

The best place to let a group through is on the green. Mark your balls, step aside, and wave the group through. Then, while they are making their way to the green, go ahead and putt out. You can then move to the next tee box, where you can wait for the group to hole their putts and let them go ahead off the next tee. That way, you haven't held up play. You've just reordered the foursomes. That's the idea. Don't let a group play through just because you're looking for a lost ball. If you've looked until play has backed up behind you, you've spent too much time looking already. Let it go. Anytime you let a group play through in the middle of a hole, you're disrupting traffic.

And that's poor etiquette.

Should you find yourself stuck behind a slow group, resist the temptation to get angry. They may not know they are holding you up. Never, ever hit into the group in front of you. That only raises tensions and creates ugly situations. Instead, wait for an opportunity when you can speak with the group and ask if you can play through at the next tee or on the next green. They'll almost always say yes if you approach the situation with kindness. If they are out of position and fail to let you through, consult a course ranger or the head professional. Taking matters into your own hands can only lead to trouble.

A FEW WORDS ON CELL PHONES

As the world changes, so does the game of golf. Wireless communication has changed the way that business operates, and it's changed the way we live. One of the products of all this change is that more and more people now bring cellular phones with them onto the golf course.

I've heard all kinds of opinions about cell phones on the course. The fact of the matter is that they're here to stay, so we have to integrate their use into the etiquette of the game. I think it's wonderful that people who might not otherwise be able to get out and spend an afternoon on the golf course can now do it because of this technology. I'll make the same argument for the use of golf carts. Yes, I miss the days of everybody walking, but I'm happy that golf carts allow people to keep on playing golf well into the later years of their lives.

There's no reason for cell phones to bother anyone on a golf course if the owners of these phones would follow a few simple rules. I don't know if anyone else has done it or not, but here's my proposal for cell phone etiquette on the golf course:

1. **DON'T RECEIVE INCOMING CALLS.** If you bring your cell phone to the course, you should know how to use voice mail and caller ID to get an idea of who is trying to reach you without annoying your fellow players with a ringing telephone.

2. **DON'T HOLD UP PLAY.** If the cell phone is causing you to be unprepared to play your shot when it's your turn, then you are displaying poor etiquette. Get out of the golf cart and walk to your ball, using that time to make your phone call. Make the person on the other end of the phone wait while you play your shot. On the golf course, respect for your fellow players is more important than the convenience of the person on the other end of the line.

3. **STEP AWAY FROM YOUR GROUP.** The members of your group didn't ask you to bring the phone with you. If you use it politely, it shouldn't bother them. But when you hold a conversation right in the middle of your foursome, you make them feel like they have to be quiet in order not to disturb you. Step away so they can carry on as they normally would on the course.

I don't see any excuse for poor etiquette. Learn the basics of moving around the course quickly and pleasantly. Then make sure that you're always asking yourself how your actions are affecting those around you. If you do that, people should always enjoy playing golf with you.

KNOWLEDGE IS POWER

I'll give you this piece of advice: go out and buy the *Rules of Golf.* Then study it, particularly if you ever plan to play in competitions. The USGA conducts workshops all around the country every year. Attend one. By knowing the rules, you will know the game as all the greats have played it, and you will become a custodian of the most honorable sport on earth.

I am disturbed by the lack of rules awareness apparent today on the PGA Tour. Davis Love III ended up being disqualified at the 1997 Players Championship after accidentally hitting his ball while taking a practice stroke with his putter. Love didn't know that the rules

called for him to return his ball to its original position with a penalty of one stroke. Instead, he took a one-stroke penalty and played the ball from its new position. Failure to replace the ball carries a separate penalty. Love ended up signing an incorrect scorecard and being disqualified because of his lack of knowledge. Amazingly, neither his caddie, nor his fellow competitor, nor the PGA Tour officials with the group noticed the secondary infraction.

I am reminded every day of the importance of knowing the rules. The reminder is a small sliver of wood that hangs on the wall of my house. It was a gift to me from my friend Craig Stadler, and it came from the tree that starred in one of golf's most bizarre rulings ever.

Stadler was in the thick of contention on Saturday afternoon at the 1987 Andy Williams Open, played at Torrey Pines Golf Course in La Jolla, California. On the 14th hole, he pushed his tee shot to the right of the fairway, and the ball came to rest under a tree. Stadler has always been an imaginative player, and rather than take an unplayable lie penalty, he decided to play the shot from a kneeling position. Now, any of you who have traveled to the San Diego area in the winter know that you can get showers from time to time. The ground was damp, and Stadler neatly folded a towel, knelt on it, and played a great shot back to the fairway. He finished the round, signed his scorecard, and came to the golf course on Sunday ready to play for the title.

Craig did play on Sunday, eventually finishing second in the tournament. Unfortunately for him, however, NBC had been replaying the towel shot from the day before throughout the final-round telecast. A viewer who saw the highlights of Saturday's round on TV called the PGA Tour rules official at the scene and explained that according to the *Rules of Golf,* the towel represented "building a stance" through artificial means—a clear violation of rule 133. Stadler may only have tried to keep his pants dry, but the rules are the rules. The Tour assessed him a penalty, thereby changing his score for that hole. Because he had already signed his scorecard with an incorrect lower score, he was disqualified from the tournament. His lack of knowledge of the rules had cost him $37,000.

Later, Stadler confessed that he had not sat down and read the *Rules of Golf* in some time. He vowed to do it and did, and he has stayed free of controversy and had a very successful career since then—even winning a few years ago on that same Torrey Pines course. When the operators of Torrey Pines decided a couple of years ago to remove the tree from the 14th hole, they called Stadler to fire up the chainsaw and do the honors, which he was happy to do.

Shortly after that, I got my piece of the tree.

WALK THROUGH THE FRONT DOOR

Golf is an invitation to join the greatest club of all. When you play golf—particularly when you play with pride and etiquette and work to sharpen your skills—you'll meet all types of people. More than that, you'll get to know these people. That's why golf is so important to business. It's not so much that big deals get made on the course—those deals generally take time and effort that you'd rather not steal from your golf game. But golf gives businesspeople the chance to build even better relationships with their clients and colleagues. You don't have to be a great player to reap these benefits. You just have to respect and love the game. My brother, Dabney, has played golf for many years. He's not the best ball striker in the world, but his putting has made him a valuable member of many scramble teams, and that's been a big plus for his business.

Golf won't necessarily make you a success in business or in life, but it can give you a great head start. On the golf course, the CEO and the mail-room clerk are on equal footing. They shed their roles and play a game they love.

When they come together at the 19th hole, they've gained a little understanding about each other as people, not as titles. That's what I mean when I say that golf lets you go in the front door. Your love for the game will leave an impression with everyone you ever meet on the golf course, and making a good impression never hurt anyone.

The community of golf has a heart of gold. Is there any other sport that devotes so much time and energy to raising money for charities? From local tournaments to the PGA Tour, golfers come together and use their enthusiasm for the game to make contributions to their cities and to the less fortunate. Golf is a privilege and a gift that we've been lucky enough to share. It's up to us to make sure that the gift does some good for others.

LOVE THE COURSE

There are a lot of great games in the world. I've loved baseball and football all my life. I'm sure that I could learn to love soccer, cricket, rugby, or tennis. But golf is the greatest game of all. And one of the greatest things about the game is that we play it on golf courses. No two golf courses are alike. They don't rest on the land. They are the land. Golf courses change with the seasons. They recede in the fall as the color fades from the fairways and the trees, and they reemerge in the spring. Think of how you feel when you see the green grass returning. Golf courses mature with age. Trees grow and change the strategies of certain holes. These qualities make golf courses the most magnificent sporting venues on earth, places capable of inspiring a quiet reverence or a thrilling sense of exhilaration. When I look back on my life in golf, I remember the golf courses just as I remember the faces of all the friends I've made in the game.

Golfers spend too much energy trying to master the particulars of the golf swing, the putting stroke, or the other technical parts of the game. I think you should start your search for lower scores simply by loving the golf course. When you're on the course, you're spending quality time with your friends and family in a beautiful setting. You're doing something you love to do. If there's one mistake I see people make over and over, it's that they treat golf like work. We call it *playing* golf for a reason. Don't get me wrong—

anytime you commit yourself to anything, you should take it seriously and try to do it as well as you can. But golf isn't a matter of life and death. It's only a matter of life and of living.

I say a little prayer of thanks every time I step onto the first tee. Golf is a gift, and the golf course is the wrapping. Think of how you feel when you receive a present. It's not always what's inside the box that matters, it's the spirit of the moment. I want you to see golf as a celebration and a search for beauty, not a quest for perfection.

TAKE REFUGE

We live most of our lives on concrete. That's where we work, where we drive, where we do our hectic thinking and planning. If you love golf, the golf course is your refuge from all of that. I knew Mickey Mantle practically his whole life. Only on the golf course did he ever truly relax. You could see the tension drain out of him as soon as he stepped onto the first tee. On the course, you know that you will get the space to pursue your game without all the interruptions of the concrete world. You're a member of a global club.

I've never understood why people put so much pressure on themselves to perform. You don't put pressure on yourself to enjoy the beach or to savor a quiet evening in the mountains. You just feed off the beauty of the environment. Performance in golf comes from feeling that you're an extension of the golf course. All you have to do is move that little ball around from place to place. You're going to have a bad round every now and then, but you need to ask yourself some hard questions if you let a bad round turn into a bad day. Walter Hagen said to "stop and smell the flowers." What he meant was that you shouldn't put so much pressure on your game. Imagine a golf course in the early morning. The dew is shining in the sunlight. You smell the freshly cut grass. The birds are singing all around you, and the people who are with you are there because they share your love of the game. If you can't sit at your desk and feel more peaceful with those images, then you should find another pastime. Now why should you block all of that out by thinking of nothing but your golf game when you arrive at the course?

I've played hundreds of golf courses in my life, and I've found something to love about every one of them. It's an honor to play a fine golf course. You get to walk on history. You can't go play catch at Yankee Stadium, but I played the West Course at Winged Foot Golf Club just after Davis Love III won the PGA Championship there. As I came up to the final hole, I couldn't help but imagine how he must have felt only a few days earlier. I thought of him and how proud his late father, a famous golf instructor I knew quite well, must have been, watching from the clouds. I thought about the rainbow that appeared as Love raised his arms in his first major championship victory, and it gave me shivers. Golf is unique among all sports in that it gives you the chance to test your own game on the very same courses that decide the most famous tournaments in the world.

Of course, you'll strike history at any golf course if you dig a little. When I was younger I used to play a lot of golf at Baxter Springs Golf and Country Club in Baxter Springs, Kansas. The course is only nine holes and will never host a U.S. Open or be featured in a *Golf Digest* ranking, but I witnessed history there. In those days the greens at Baxter Springs were sand greens with an oil base. You actually had to run a drag across the line of your putt to smooth out the surface. I often played there with a very good friend of mine who was a member, and sometimes his young son would join us for a few holes. I was so impressed with the youngster's swing and natural understanding of the game that on one of my visits to Baxter Springs I brought him a set of four cut-down clubs. Little did I know that I would later see that same boy win three U.S. Open titles (including one at Winged Foot). His name was Hale Irwin.

FIND THE BEAUTY

History, tradition, and natural setting come together in a golf course as they do nowhere else. When people ask me about my favorite courses, I have to stop and think. There's nothing more beautiful than seaside golf. The ocean stretches out forever, and there you are, playing on the edge of the world. Mountain golf can take your breath away with its scenic views. Then again, you could never

beat the beauty of our own little club here in Miami, Oklahoma. The trees and the wind that blows in from the plains make sweet music for sure, and should you post an under-par score, the club members will have you sign Dr. W. D. Jackson's old hat that hangs in the bag room. You then become a part of the history and tradition of our club. Well, you get the picture. If you look for the beauty in any golf course, you'll find it. And when you find it, you've done more for your game than any amount of lessons ever could do. You've put things in perspective.

My favorite story of finding the beauty of a golf course is the story of Bobby Jones and his first visit to the Royal and Ancient Golf Club of St. Andrews. Jones was just a teenager—obsessed as all teenagers are with trying to control his surroundings—when he visited the Old Course for the first time. There, the future king of the game encountered a landscape and course design he had never seen. To say that he failed to appreciate it at first would be an understatement. In fact, in his first competitive round, he got caught in a pot bunker. Rather than take his medicine and play out sideways, he chose to flail away in an unsuccessful attempt to advance the ball. After posting a double-digit number on the hole, he stormed off the course and back to the clubhouse. There he received a warning, in no uncertain terms, that such behavior would not be tolerated ever again in a Royal and Ancient competition. That incident did more to make Jones a complete player than anything else in his career. He learned to stop fighting the golf course and start learning how to play it as it was. Jones returned to win an Open Championship on the storied links of St. Andrews, and in his later years, he often remarked that if he could play only one course for the rest of his life, St. Andrews would be his choice. He found the beauty of the golf course, and it made him a better player.

Finding the beauty of a golf course sometimes means letting go of your ego. One of the most common sources of frustration that I see among golfers is that they don't play the course as it's meant to be played. Usually it's because they don't play the proper set of tees. Why on earth would an 18-handicapper want to ever play a course from the championship tees? It's very hard to find beauty when you spend all your time looking for balls because you can't reach the fairway from the tee. Select the tees that the architect meant for golfers of your skill level. Then play the course to the best of your ability. You'll have more fun, you'll find more beauty, and you'll play better golf.

DO YOUR PART

In order to find beauty on the golf course, you need to respect beauty. Keeping a golf course in good condition requires a lot of work. Just ask any superintendent. We've come to expect our golf courses to be just about perfect, but that perfection doesn't happen overnight. You'd be shocked to see how early the grounds crew gets started every morning just so you will have a well-manicured course to enjoy. That's why you have to pitch in by making sure that you leave the golf course in the same great shape in which you found it, if not better. Some people call this "responsibility." I call it common courtesy toward your fellow golfers, and it's just as important as the etiquette of playing golf.

I don't think there's anything more pathetic than a beautiful putting surface covered with ball marks. If you're fortunate enough to make a ball mark, that means you're usually right around the green. To get to repair a ball mark is an achievement that you can savor and enjoy. Watch the pros. They make a ritual of repairing their pitch marks. You should, too. Always carry a ball mark tool, or, better yet, collect them from every course you play so that you'll always have some extras in case someone in your group is without one.

Make sure you repair pitch marks correctly by digging in at the edges and pulling the meat of the mark toward the front. The idea is to lay the grass back over the ball mark so that the repaired mark is unobtrusive. If you start in the center of the mark and dig too deeply, you'll simply pull sand up from underneath the roots of the grass, and then you've only made the problem worse. If you have holed out and are waiting for other players to finish putting, repair another mark or two off to the side so that you've left the green in even better condition than you found it.

Along these same lines, replace your divots in the fairway. If the course you're playing provides a dirt and seed mixture, use it. Otherwise, take the few seconds to collect your divot, replacing it properly by aligning the grain of the grass on the divot to the grain of the fairway. It surely won't take you long to start cursing other golfers when you hit a perfect drive that ends up smack in the middle of a deep divot. Don't let yourself be the target of someone else's curses.

Obey the cart-path rules, even when you don't understand them. If there's a "cart path only" rule or a "90-degree" rule, it's because the superintendent is trying to protect the fairway from damage caused by the weight of the cart. Always put the good of the golf course above your own personal convenience. Besides, if you're young and healthy you should be walking the course anyway!

Finally, learn how to rake the bunkers. Would you trust a person who didn't clean up his mess in the kitchen before you came to start cooking? Of course not. It's just as rude on the golf course to leave a bunker unraked. The players behind you don't want to be playing out of your footprints or sand divots. All it takes is a couple of seconds to smooth out the sand's surface so that your fellow golfers will have a chance to get up and down.

If you already follow these course maintenance guidelines, see if there are ways that you could do them better. And always help teach new players—and careless veterans—the importance. You belong to the community of golfers, and your golf course reflects on that community. Show a little pride in it.

CROSS THE GENERATION GAP

Very little in this world stays the same. In the 70 years that I've been playing golf, I've seen wars come and go, fortunes won and lost, cities rise and fall. Sometimes I think it would be impossible to digest the change going on around me all the time if I didn't have golf. The game's importance, values, lessons, and memories constantly keep things in and around my life in perspective.

Golf may not have kept me from growing older, but it sure has kept me from feeling old. The game has kept me young because it's kept me in touch with kids. No other sport brings the generations together the way golf does. When I was a boy, Oklahoma was still a rough-and-ready frontier. I learned its history on the golf course, playing with old-timers who had seen the birth of the state. We were friends, those older folks and me. Every morning I would sling my clubs over my shoulder and board a Greyhound bus in Quapaw, paying a dime for the short ride to Baxter Springs, Kansas. I'd stay until it was dark. The lessons I learned on those long summer days have stayed with me forever, and they have turned into lessons for the thousands of kids I've had the great fortune of knowing and teaching all these years.

People ask me all the time when they should start their kids at golf, and I tell them, "as soon as they show an interest in it." The family that plays together stays together. That's been my experience. In a world that moves as quickly as ours does today, there are very few activities that allow you to spend four hours of true quality time with the people you love. Golf fills those four hours with so many opportunities for sharing, learning, and growing. Children who play golf with their parents will look forward to spending time with their parents for the rest of their lives. Even as you grow through the trying times of adolesence and young adulthood, the golf course will give you the chance to retreat from the pressures of living and just enjoy being together. And isn't that what a family is all about?

Because of the young people I've known through golf, I've never worried about the future. I know we're going to be just fine. In a lot of ways, they've taught me as much as I've taught them, and I think these kids yearn for the tradition and history that golf provides. I consider golf a gift, one that you can give to your children and their children. Not only is golf a great activity that they'll enjoy all their lives, but it has a code of values and ethics they can live by. I still start all my junior lessons by letting the kids know that they'll use "sir" and "ma'am" when talking with the adults they meet through golf. Golf provides a living classroom for teaching discipline and hard work, achievement, and the graceful handling of loss. Remember that kids are born into this world with no direction. They depend on you to give it to them. Introducing a kid to golf is your chance to open up a world of possibilities.

Golf teaches kids to be "people smart." It breaks down the walls between generations. Every golf course has a few colorful characters who just want to be a part of the young people who are learning the game. They watch over them, helping them learn golf skills, reproaching them for violations of the rules or for losing their tempers. They tell them the stories that all golfers should know—the legends of great players and bygone times. Go home and watch the news on your television tonight. Kids today have to deal with too much of the negative. Golf—and the people they meet through the game—offers something more positive.

Beyond all of that, golf requires dedication and energy, something kids just naturally possess. When a youngster is serious about improving his or her golf game, there's not a lot of time for trouble. Kids play all day and look forward to playing well the next day. That's a mighty strong incentive for staying off the streets. The confidence kids get from being a part of something as difficult and rewarding as golf will carry over into everything they do. I've never been afraid of anyone or any situation where I had to mix with people I didn't know. I credit golf for that.

Finally, golf is forever. You already know that—that's why you're reading this book. When you give a child the gift of golf, you're giving something that will last a lifetime. I always encouraged my kids to play other sports like football, baseball, and basketball. Those sports teach many lessons as well, but you can't play them forever. Golf, on the other hand, will always be there.

I'm 80 years old, and there's not a day that goes by that I don't find out something new about myself thanks to golf. Similary, every round adds something to my soapbox repertoire. I hope you've found something in these pages to take with you as you continue your journey through the greatest game of all.

I know I have.

AFTERWORD

WE'VE COVERED A LOT OF GROUND IN THIS BOOK, AND I KNOW IT'S A LOT TO DIGEST.

If you know anything about me, you know I'm all about the hands-on approach. This is why we featured so many photographs in this book—it's awfully hard to pick up a swing key without at least seeing a picture or two. I hope we did a good job.

If you desire even more one-on-one instruction, then visit www.kiss-golf.com. There you'll find even more tips and some video lessons that coincide with a lot of the instruction contained in this text. Also, if you have any questions about your swing or golf technique in general, you can email me through the site, and I'll get back to you as soon as I'm able. I'm just now learning how to use the computer, but I'm getting pretty handy at it.

Of course, you can catch some of my newer tips and swing thoughts in upcoming issues of *Golf Tips* magazine. You can buy *Golf Tips* at your local newsstand. If you wish to subscribe, visit the magazine's website, www.golftipsmag.com. I've been asked to write for all the other major golf publications, but I'd have nothing to do with them. If you're a serious golfer, then *Golf Tips* is the magazine for you.

Finally, I'd be remiss if I didn't talk about my equipment. Right now I have in my bag some Nike irons (www.nikegolf.com), a putter and some wedges from De La Cruz Golf (www.delacruzgolf.com), and a great driver and fairway wood from Tour Edge (www.touredge.com). Finding the right gear is an important first step in improving your game. Start your search with the products I use—they're some of the best around.

Good luck with everything. I hope you become the golfer you want to be. This is a great game, folks, and it has given me so many fantastic moments. It only gets better when you can make a few more birdies and a lot fewer bogeys.